TRAILBLAZING WITH GOD

Learning to Walk on the Water

JANE ANN DERR

PRESS

Trailblazing With God
Learning to Walk on the Water
by Jane Ann Derr

Printed in the United States of America

ISBN 978-1-60477-866-3

Unless otherwise indicated, Bible quotations are taken from The New King James Version. Copyright © 1982 by Thomas Nelson, Inc. Used by Permission.

www.xulonpress.com

DEDICATION

This book is dedicated to my precious husband, Harold. God gave him to me as a great gift. I will always miss him. He passed away September 18, 2006, but I will always be grateful for the wonderful fifty-five years that we shared together, and I will cherish all of my precious memories.

I shared many exciting adventures with Harold. One of these adventures was our journey to Ghana, West Africa. We had been working on this book together as he fought his year-long battle with cancer. I promised him I would finish this book. So through many prayers of loved ones and tear-stained pages, I have finally completed this task.

CONTENTS

INTRODUCTION

The purpose of this book is to show that God can use ordinary people with all of their warts and flaws. He changes willing, weak people by the power of the Holy Spirit, who is none other than the power of the risen Christ. These examples show how God can use anyone for His Divine purpose. However, we must choose to be used, attentively listen and obey His call. We must focus on God and not our flaws.

All of the Apostles had their issues, but God used them. Paul was a murderer and God transformed his life into the dynamic servant who wrote most of the New Testament Books. So no matter your background, God can use you. The choice is up to you.

Harold told the children many times that we were not following a path, but we were blazing a trail like his grandfather, John Forsyth. Grandpa Forsyth took his family from Indiana to Kansas in a covered wagon in the late eighteen hundreds to homestead Kansas. He was a farmer who wanted more land to support his large family.

The flat, grassy plains of Kansas had no road markers. So Grandpa Forsyth steered a straight course by looking back at the tracks the wagon had made as it traveled over the grass. If you look forward, you travel in a circle, if you look back, you steer a straight course.

We grow in Christ as we thoughtfully and thankfully look back to where we were before Christ came into our life, and where we are now.

ACKNOWLEDGMENTS

Thinking back, this book has been a work in progress since 1965. My mother carefully saved all of our letters and gave them back to me when we returned to California. My last real conversation with Mother before she died in 1971 consisted of many strong encouraging words about why I should write this book. She insisted that I promise her I would write this. After many unsuccessful attempts were made to move this project forward, urgent needs always forced me to again file away my bits and pieces and wait.

Circumstances then changed for us in 2005 when health concerns forced Harold to retire from preaching. At that time, we started working diligently and prayerfully on this book. However, this effort was short-lived due to frequent trips to the doctor and hospital, painful chemo treatments and finally his passing from this life September 18, 2006. Again I made a promise to Harold that I would complete this book with God's help.

Within a very short time, God started sending people my way to fulfill this dream. Our five children sent me daily calls of encouragement urging me to keep on writing. They have patiently read all the letters, journals, drafts and numerous re-writes, made valuable suggestions and shared their insights. Our son-in-law Tim White, who was not with us on the Ghana journey, shared our book writing journey by giving valuable suggestions such as, "I want to hear what you left out." So God gave our family a great opportunity to go on another journey together.

After all of these years, all five children have said that going on our adventure to Ghana was the best gift we could have given them. It changed their lives. They also have said that they have been so blessed by going back and taking this journey again together with adult eyes.

Judy Miller's sweet spirit has been a great encouragement to me. She read the first drafts, made suggestions and kept me going with her love and prayers. Leon and Ruth Gibson have also read drafts, prayed for me and encouraged me.

This book would never have been, without our dear sweet friends Dr. Henry Farrar and his wonderful wife Grace. They spent many hours reading the drafts, and making many valuable suggestions. Grace's words of encouragement were priceless! Rees and Patti Bryant had saved letters that Harold had written to Rees 42 years ago and they sent them to me May 2007. Jerry Reynolds has been a great encourager and sent me valuable current information. Many at Grace Chapel Church of Christ have faithfully encouraged and prayed for me as well as many at Etowah River Church of Christ and many others—their names would fill many pages. I am grateful to God for each one.

In & Out Photo and Digital Imaging was a tremendous help with the photos for the book. I could not thank them enough. You can check out their website at www.inandoutphoto.com. I accidentally dropped my billfold on the floor in their store after I left. I had no idea the billfold was lost for two days. When I finally checked my voice mail, Mike from In & Out Photo had left a message on my voice mail saying that they were keeping my billfold in their office for safekeeping until I came in! When I got the billfold everything was just as I had left it. I thanked them and thanked God for taking care of me again!

Collecting information for the book has been like going to a big family reunion and re-connecting with people you love but haven't seen in a long time. It reminds me what Heaven must be like—each sharing stories of our battles and praising God for our victory in Jesus Christ.

FORWARD

"It has been our privilege to know Jane Ann Derr ever since she and her family came from Ghana to visit us at our mission compound in Nigeria in 1965. At that time mission work for the Derrs was very difficult due to the Communist activities in Ghana. Food was scarce. Travel and speech were restricted, and the press was violently anti-American. The Derrs were determined to go back to their chosen mission field and to stay as long as it was possible to do so. We shared some fervent prayer sessions with Jane Ann and Harold before they left to return to Ghana. Since then we have held them in the highest regard. Jane Ann's readers will see how God gave this woman of faith the power to overcome as she faced some extraordinary obstacles."

Rees and Patti Bryant
Former missionaries to Nigeria
Kissimmee, Florida

"Most of us cannot travel abroad to share our faith—yet through this book, you will be motivated to reach out to those who are <u>near</u> —Those who need Jesus, as Lord of Life." With much love and prayers,

Judy Miller
Widow of Jule Miller and Author of 19 books
Pasadena, Texas

"We both found this book quite interesting, reflecting faith, dedication and perseverance—especially in Harold. A brave man, that Harold."

Ruth and Robert Leon Gibson
Author
Santa Ana, California

PART ONE

The Journey Begins

"I heard the voice of the Lord saying: 'Whom shall I send, and
who will go for Us?' Then I said, "Here am I! Send me."
(Isaiah 6:8-9)

September 7, 1963, I reluctantly stepped out of the Pan Am DC8
Jet. I squinted hard to get my first glimpse of Ghana, West
Africa. The brightness of the sun nearly blinded me. I squinted hard
to see because everything looked so black to me at first. As soon as
I could see clearly, I caught a glimpse of a flag—red, yellow, and
green with a large black star in the middle. Instantly, my stomach
knotted at the absence of our own red, white and blue. The realization of where we actually were hit hard. We had burned our bridges.
Now we were here. There was no turning back. The hot mid-day
sun beat down on the back of my neck. I labored to breathe as the
hot, humid air overwhelmed me. The air reeked of charcoal burning
smoke mingled with a musty overlay. Then a sweet scent filled my
nostrils –like a field of jasmine beginning to bloom. The strap of the
camera bag slipped on my arm and gave me a jolt. I grabbed the rail
tightly to catch my balance. I swallowed hard, straightened the strap
of the camera bag, and carefully descended the stairs of the ramp to
the ground below.

I turned around and saw Harold and the children standing at the
top of the ramp. My heart swelled with pride as I saw my thirty-

three-year-old, adventurous husband with his jet black curly hair blowing in the breeze. He always stood so tall and erect with his shoulders back like an Indian chief. I could see his calm brown eyes and radiant smile, comforting the children and lining them up, to make their orderly descent down the ramp. He had insisted on following behind me to make sure that he had retrieved our entire luggage. Debbie, our twelve-year-old, was the oldest. She cautiously stepped down while at the same time looking around with great curiosity. Diana, our ten-year-old stood tall and erect like her Daddy. She hurriedly bounced down the steps pushing Debbie to walk faster. Following behind was nine-year-old Janice. She took her time as she drank in all of the exotic sights, smells and sounds. Looking scared, six-year-old Cathy hid behind her Daddy. After a reassuring hug, she very slowly and carefully inched down the steps. Four-year-old John held his Daddy's hand very tightly and followed Cathy. Harold took a quick look to survey the new landscape. His face lit up with a glowing smile as he ushered the children down the ramp. He tightened his grip on the heavy, bulging red leather suitcase and descended down the stairs.

"How do you like it, sweetheart? What do you think?" he asked as his face lit up in a glowing smile.

Cathy, Diana, Debbie, John and Jane Ann in front of our Pan Am DC8 Jet. Janice decided to help her Daddy take the picture.

As I gazed at our surroundings, I saw a vivid array of bright, vibrant colors; fuchsia, royal blue, gold, and white garments draped gracefully around strong, athletic bodies with deep mahogany shaded skin. Everyone was busily rushing around. Looking up, I could see a very deep blue sky with sharp contrasts of white fluffy clouds drifting by. The soil was deep burnt orange clay and the foliage on the trees, shrubs and flowers were a deep blue green. I could hear drumming and singing.

Yesterday, I remembered watching, as the drab concrete and steel structures peered through the lonely clouds that wandered across the pale blue sky and faded into the distance when our jet soared away from the jagged shores of America. Wow! What a contrast!

"Well – uh—it's different." I smiled faintly. *As a young girl, I had prayed to marry a preacher never dreaming I would be here. I do enjoy remembering that time thirteen years ago, when I was a seventeen-year-old bride. That was a different time. This is now.*

Harold reached over and tenderly clasped my hand in his. I looked up at his calm brown eyes and surveyed his radiant smile as he whispered, "I love you, sweetheart. You will always be my beautiful bride."

Just then a large dilapided bus screeched its brakes and stopped near us. It was empty except for the African driver. We all stepped up into the bus and sat down on the torn leather seats near the front door. Turning my head toward the window I could see the two flight attendants, the pilot and the co-pilot in their neat blue Pan Am uniforms. They laughed together as they walked toward the bus. Just as soon as they hopped on, the bus pulled away rattling noisily as it went. In a few minutes the bus jolted to a squeaky stop. We parked in front of the terminal with Accra signage over the front door. We jumped down out of the bus and walked toward the terminal. A strange feeling erupted in me as I realized that we were the only white people in sight. As I listened, I heard strange words. Suddenly I realized that I couldn't understand a word that people were saying.

Three tall muscular policemen in black uniforms met us at the door. In a very businesslike manner one policeman barked, "Where is your passport?" Although he spoke English, it was very difficult to understand. Harold hesitated.

Setting the suitcase and camera bag down, Harold handed the packet of papers to him. After several minutes of deliberation, the policeman, who seemed to be in charge, smiled and ushered us inside saying, "We welcome you to Ghana." Harold took the packet of papers and stuffed them inside his suit jacket pocket.

Inside the terminal we were guided to another entry point. This consisted of a large desk cluttered with stacks of files and papers scattered about. A policeman behind the desk greeted us asking Harold again for our passport, visa and other documents. After several long minutes of studying all of our papers, the policeman stamped several pages. He handed the packet back to Harold saying, "We hope you will have an enjoyable two years in Ghana. We welcome all Americans to beautiful Ghana. Take your baggage to the counter on the other side of the terminal. The customs officials will inspect your baggage and then you can be on your way."

Just as soon as the customs officials checked the baggage and nodded their heads, six young men grabbed the handle of the suitcase at the same time and pulled and tugged mercilessly. After a stern reprimand from the customs official, all but one young man let loose of the suitcase. The other young men followed closely behind the one young man as he ran with the suitcase. We followed to the other side of the building where he set the suitcase on a counter. Turning to face Harold, the frail young man's face lit up with a broad smile exposing his white shining teeth, as he said, "Dash me!" and held out his hand.

"Harold, what is he talking about?"

"Can't you figure that out?" Harold laughed as he reached into his pocket and pulled out a large unfamiliar silver coin with a picture of Kwame Nkrumah on it and gave it to the young man.

"Madasi Pii!" he said as he ran away.

Looking at the white uniformed man behind the counter, Harold said, "Please, sir, will you tell me when our plane leaves for Kumasi?"

"Oh, sir, are you the Harold Derr family? I have reservations for you on the next plane. If you will kindly be patient a few minutes, the plane will be leaving shortly. Please wait in those chairs by the wall."

We all walked directly over to the faded green canvas chairs. The children were very quiet and seemed overwhelmed with all the new sights, sounds and smells. I looked sorrowfully at the dusty chairs and could just picture the fine red clay dust that covered the chair ruining my pretty new dress. Just then Harold caught a glimpse of my perplexing situation. He took a handkerchief out of his pocket, knocked the top layer of dust out of the chair and motioned for me to sit down. "Come on, sweetheart. Sit here by me."

He seemed to sense my uneasiness. Reaching over and gently holding my hand, he whispered, "I love you. You will always be my beautiful bride." *As he gazed into my eyes, I began to feel that everything was going to be all right.*

Looking around we were reminded again that we were the only white people in the crowded room. Suddenly we became acutely aware that it was going to be very difficult to adjust to our new environment. We listened intently to all of the strange sounds around us: the swishing of bare feet across the dirty brown tile floor; the crying of hungry children; the barking of the policemen and the customs officials; people everywhere talking with a mixture of different languages; a loud speaker blaring sounds in many unfamiliar languages then repeating in English the flight arrivals. We noticed that most of the flights were late, and the time of our flight kept changing. Harold looked over at us and saw that we too were quite absorbed in observing our new surrounding.

"Hey, gang, are you thirsty?" Harold said as he listened to the jazzy music drifting in from the patio of the hotel across the street.

"Yes, it's so hot here." I replied as I brushed the perspiration off of my brow. "Could you get us a cold drink somewhere?"

Quite curious to find out what was outside, Harold replied, "Hear that music across the street? Stay here and I'll go see if I can find us some refreshing lemonade."

As Harold left the building, my eyes followed him every step of the way. All at once I felt a pang of uneasiness sweep over me as I looked across the room and saw not one familiar sight. Just then the man in the white uniform that had spoken with us about our plane reservations walked up to the blackboard on the wall across the room and erased the time of our flight. Looking up over the blackboard, I could see the large clock. It was 2:00 P.M. The pang of uneasiness turned into fear as I noticed that everywhere many policemen wandered around the room aimlessly. This reminded me of the stories that I had read about Ghana and the dictator, President Kwame Nkrumah, who ruled Ghana with an iron hand imprisoning all who dared to oppose him. Turning my head aimlessly from side to side my eyes stopped at a large picture of "Big Brother", Nkrumah. He was clad in his bright colored Roman draped toga. As I saw his stern face looking at me, I started to panic. *Why? Why doesn't Harold hurry with those cold drinks?* The children all sat very quietly looking around mesmerized by the new sights.

As I surveyed the room wishfully searching for Harold's familiar form to appear, a strange sight caught my attention. Nearby and in the middle of the room, I saw an African family consisting of one man and three women. The women were probably his wives and his seven children. All were standing around him. Most of the children looked dirty and hungry and several were naked. The oldest looking woman in the group reached up to her head. She then lifted a large bundle of something all tied together in a colored blue and white cloth. Then she set the bundle on the dirty brown tile floor. As she opened up her African suitcase bundle to hunt for something, I scanned through some of the contents: pots and pans; large tubular yams; a machete; a kerosene lantern; an old model portable sewing machine with a crank-type wheel on the side; a neatly folded stack of brightly colored cloth; a charcoal firepot; a charcoal iron; red peppers and something that looked like large green bananas. Just then the woman pulled out some smoked fish and handed it to the children. One of the other women opened up the blue granite pan she was carrying on her head and set it down on the floor. The children all gathered around the pan and dipped the smoked fish into the red greasy, oily mixture and my stomach turned flip flops as the aroma of the smoked fish mixture drifted our way.

I stood up to see if I could find Harold. As I started to leave, Harold entered the room carrying seven green bottles of some kind of a drink. As soon as he saw me he started grinning from ear to ear.

"Sorry I was gone so long, honey. But you will never guess what a difficult time I had getting this."

"Why? What's so difficult about getting a cold drink?"

"Plenty!" he chuckled.

"Come on. Tell me what happened."

"They don't call it 'soda pop'. It's 'drinkables' or 'minerals', he laughed.

"Minerals! Why minerals?"

"Who knows why, honey? That's just the way it is. If you want a drink, call it "minerals", Harold replied as he handed the bottle to me and then gave the children bottles.

"Is this lemonade?"

"Well, no," he laughed, "but let's just call it good ole American 7-Up". He then took a long drink from the bottle.

"Daddy, this tastes funny," said Diana.

"It's cold. Just drink it."

"Did they have any other flavors?" said Debbie as she frowned.

I carried my bottle back to the canvas chair, sat down and reached into my purse to pull out a clean white handkerchief. Carefully I wiped the top of the bottle. After drinking a little sip, I muttered, "It does sort of taste like 7-Up," as I tried to smile.

"Harold, when you were gone they changed the time of our flight again. Would you please go see about it?"

"Oh, honey, please give me a minute to rest before I have to go through all of that palaver again."

"What do you mean 'palaver'?"

"Oh, never mind. Forget it," he said as he placed the empty bottle on the floor and sauntered toward the desk across the room. As I looked at the expression on his face, I could see his frown and wondered if he was thinking about the difficult experience he had just encountered trying to communicate with the clerk in order to just get cold drinks.

A few minutes after eight o'clock that evening, we boarded a very small propeller plane, a DC-3. It looked like an old cast off from World War Two. As we settled down into the small bucket-type seats and looked around, we found little in this plane to resemble the super jet that we had been on before. Tiny rubber fans about five inches in diameter were placed over each seat to replace the vast air conditioning system on the jet. I remembered what this plane looked like from the pictures I had studied in history books about the war, and I seriously wondered if this plane would get us to our destination.

As the engine started to choke and sputter, the whole plane began to vibrate and rattle. Slowly we taxied down the runway and prepared for a take-off. Just as we were ready to take off, the plane swung around and headed back toward the terminal. *Oh, no. Something is wrong and we can't fly out tonight. What shall we do? They have been expecting us since early afternoon.* The door opened and the flight attendant calmly announced that they had forgotten a passenger. We would be leaving as soon as we picked up the passenger.

I turned around to get a better look at the other passengers and to my utter dismay, I discovered that they were all laughing at this last minute irritation that would delay us at least fifteen minutes or more.

I noticed all the children were asleep, and I was so thankful how calm they have been since Harold has been with us again. They were so irritable in the Mill Creek Trailer Park in Wilmington, Delaware because their Daddy had been raising travel funds and they had missed him so much.

Looking around I noticed that we were the only white passengers on the plane. The flight attendant was now ushering the new passenger, an African woman, into a seat, and as soon as she disappeared through the door in front, the plane again taxied to the runway. As the plane took off, the engines were running at full speed. I hoped we could make it off the ground with all these people. I could feel the tires of the plane skipping across the pavement because of the weight of the passengers. Then finally by the grace of God, we were off the ground and into the air surging upward into the interior of Africa. I looked out the window. All was black except for the lights from Accra that were fading into the distance. Soon all I could see out the small window was total darkness. I looked over at Harold and started to smile. He was sound asleep and perspiration was pouring from his brow. The children were still asleep except John. He curiously looked around as he shared the seat next to me. The woman in the seat behind us had a chicken in a cage on her lap. As the chicken kept squawking, John questioned, "Mommy, how long is this flight?" he continued with, "It's sure different here than when we left New York." I turned to look again outside and to my great surprise I saw light. *Where was it coming from? Oh, no! It's lightning! A tropical storm was approaching.*

Just then a light flashed on inside the plane and I saw the sign "FASTEN YOUR SEAT BELT." "Mommy, this is fun!" John excitedly exclaimed as he peered through the window, and as we began to bounce up and down.

The pang of uneasiness swept over me again. After the bouncing continued more fiercely, John questioned, "Mommy, at first this was fun, but it's not fun anymore," he continued with a very frightened expression. "Mommy, I'm scared!"

The cold chill that permeated throughout my body was quite unaware of the hot, humid, musty atmosphere of the stuffy plane. My damp, cold hands grabbed the armrests on the seat and held on tightly. I could feel a rising sense of panic coming all over me. I gasped for breath. The air felt so heavy. *Dear God, don't let us die here.* I closed my eyes. The panicky feeling subsided and a new thought surfaced. *God I know You will protect us now after helping us narrowly escape boarding the Swissair plane that crashed killing all passengers.*

I let out a deep breath and tried to relax, but crazy thoughts kept racing through my mind as I remembered September 4 – the day that we got the call from Wendell Broom. That call changed everything. He said that the Swissair flight that we had just cancelled, crashed in Zurich and all 80 passengers were killed. My first thought at that time was: *Forgive me God for complaining and not trusting Your timing!*

The children and I had lived in our 17 foot travel trailer in Mill Creek Trailer Park in Wilmington, Delaware while Harold was still out raising funds with Jerry Reynolds. After sixteen days, Harold arrived home and reported a successful fund raising trip only to find another great challenge: our visas had not been approved yet! After many prayers, the answer was the same: one delay after another; paper got lost; need more information. The last delay meant that we had to cancel our Swissair plane reservations and re-schedule. We had been looking forward to visiting with the missionaries in Zurich and were so disappointed.

On September 4, we got the call from Wendell Broom. He read the newspaper article from Zurich, Switzerland to us saying that our flight from Zurich crashed and all 80 passengers aboard died.

The very next day our visas were approved and on September 6, we left New York on Pan American Airways that had a direct flight to Ghana. I shivered thinking about how God preserved our lives and allowed us to be in Ghana now. I took another deep breath. I thanked God for His care for us and His protection. I relaxed in my seat as I reached over and touched John's arm saying, "God will take care of us, Sweetheart. Just wait and see." *Thank you God for taking care of us.*

Just then the plane surged upward. But it was too late. We were caught in the path of a violent wind. It seemed to me that we were hanging suspended in space bouncing around for an endless eternity.

The plane bounced around in every direction. Between the rocking and rolling, I finally got up enough courage to look outside. I could see the plane's wings flapping up and down like an eagle's wings. It seemed to me that even the elements were fighting our arrival to this strange land that appeared to be another world. I looked over again at Harold. He was still asleep.

"Wake up, Harold! We're in a storm!" I said as I nudged him in the ribs.

"What! What!" he said between yawns. "Don't worry. Tropical storms are quite common here. Pilots are trained for it."

I settled back in my seat and tried to relax. As I relaxed a terrific pain swelled up in my ears. By then the children woke up crying.

"Oh, Harold, my ears! They hurt so badly. I can't stand it. What's wrong?"

"Daddy, I hurt," John sobbed as he held his ears tightly.

"Are we almost there?" Debbie asked.

"When will my ears stop hurting?" Diana asked.

"Kids, we're almost in Kumasi. Just settle down. Open your mouth wide and try to yawn and that will help," said Harold as he looked at the children from across the aisle.

Harold turned around to me and said, "The plane is not pressurized. That's why your ears hurt. Hold on. We'll be in Kumasi before long."

The storm began to subside as quickly as it started and soon the plane began to descend. I looked outside again and everything was still black.

"Harold, why are we coming down? Where are the landing lights below?"

Now, don't get so upset. I'm sure our pilot has flown this run for years. Settle down. You'll upset the children."

"I still say there are no landing lights in sight." The plane was still descending. Suddenly I felt a jolt. "What's that?"

The plane had touched the runway with a decided bounce and soon stopped. The only light that we could see outside the tiny window was a faint light from the building in the distance.

"We're here at last!"

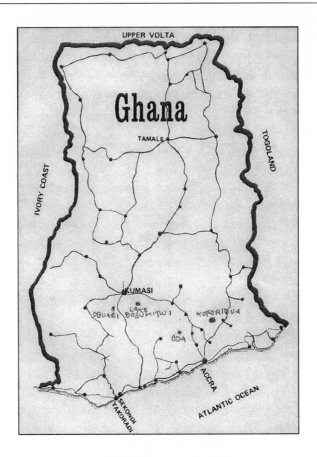

This is a map of Ghana, West Africa

When we got off the plane in Kumasi, we were met by Dwayne and Jane Davenport and a group of Ghanaian Christians. After the introductions were made and all the greetings said, we squeezed into two cars and were rushed off to the Davenports for supper. The drive through Kumasi to the Davenport's home was noisy and colorful: screeching tires; lorries filled with singing and drumming passengers; bicycles darting in and out of traffic; women walking along the road with bundles on their head and a baby tied to their back; scents of burning charcoal and a heavy sweetness permeated the air; people shouting, talking in a strange language. Soon we arrived at the Davenports. They served us a delicious meal, but it tasted different.

After supper, the Davenport's drove us to our Ghanaian home. Jane had everything in order with food in the cabinets. We quickly prepared our beds because we were so exhausted and sleepy. As I rolled and tossed on the unfamiliar firm mattress, I just could not sleep. I listened to the drums in the distance and Harold snoring. It was past midnight. The rhythmic beat of the torrential rain on the tin roof suddenly stopped. The frogs began their eerie concert in unmelodious minor chords. In the distance, slowly at first, then building up momentum, I could hear the strange chant of African drums. Talking drums. Screaming. Howling. Wailing. The nearby villagers were mourning the death of a chief. I reached over and touched Harold as he stirred slightly, gave a deep sigh, and settled back to sleep. Just knowing that he was there seemed to help me relax some. The children were so exhausted. They were all asleep.

As I started to relax, I thought about my first glimpse of this room. I shuddered when I remembered how the lizards crawling on the walls all scampered to hide behind the curtains when we lit the kerosene lantern. Tomorrow I would begin my new life in this strange land. How would I adjust? I thought about our arrival at the airport, and the small band of friendly strangers who had patiently suffered through six hours waiting for our arrival. They hadn't even taken a break for food.

Tears swelled up in my eyes as I whispered softly, *"Dear God, don't let me disappoint them. They're counting on me so much—but—but."* Then my thoughts took a twist. *I remembered my dream in Terre Haute, Indiana when I had been so sick and confused. Oh, I cannot believe this! The dream had been exactly the same scene as when we arrived in Kumasi. I had felt so happy in Africa in my dream. My heart calmed as I remembered. Then I knew God wanted me to be in Ghana. He would provide all I needed along the way.*

September 8, 1963

We woke up early the next morning to the sound of lorries rushing by on the road in front of our new home. The energetic passengers were singing, drumming, and shaking tambourines. Harold fluffed up his pillow and motioned for me to snuggle on his shoulder as we surveyed the large bedroom in the morning light.

"Do you see that big lock on the door?" I squealed!

"At last, we can have a little privacy," Harold whispered as he tickled and kissed my ear.

A loud knock on the bedroom door suddenly interrupted our gentle moment.

"Mommy, Daddy, may we come in?" Not waiting for an answer, Cathy and John opened the door and came running over to the bed.

"How did you like your new bed?" I inquired as I carefully studied their confused expressions.

"It's sure better than sleeping on that air mattress on the floor of the trailer," John recalled.

Cathy just nodded and looked around the room smiling.

Janice slipped through the door saying, "What's for breakfast? I'm hungry."

"Wake up Debbie, and I'll try to figure out what to have for breakfast," I replied.

With a satisfied expression, Janice ran out of the room.

Harold glanced at his watch on the nearby nightstand. "We do need to hurry. This is our first Sunday in Ghana, and the Davenport's will be here shortly to pick us up." Harold replied.

Worshipping for the first time in Ghana on Sunday was a very unique experience. We met in a building consisting of about six tall posts with a corrugated tin roof. The seats were benches six feet long with no backs. The congregation consisted of about fifty to sixty people –most were children. Lively lizards ran back and forth on top of the tall wall surrounding the building. Each lizard had a different colored head—green, red or orange—and their bodies stretched to about nine to twelve inches long. They looked like baby dinosaurs. However, they were very quiet for the service. The Ghanaians were very happy to have us here and treated us kindly.

The worship service was conducted about like in America. We had an assembly with songs and prayers. Next the children went to Bible Class for an hour. Afterward we had our worship service. The songs were all in Twi. Only a few of the songs we sing in America have the same words and tune as here. The people put so much expression in their singing. We all were determined to learn Twi, the native language of the Ashanti, so we can sing along with them. It is a tonal language and so different from English. The Davenports did a great job of speaking the Twi language.

Dwayne preached the sermon and B.O. Samuels was his interpreter. At the end Harold preached a short sermon and expressed to the audience how happy we were to be in Ghana. For the communion they used real wine and poor Debbie could hardly take it. She did wait until we got home to vomit. At the end of the service, we all got into a reception line and everyone came by and shook our hands to welcome us officially to Ghana. Rain in the middle of the service drenched us all.

The Amakon Church of Christ in Kumasi, Ghana. We attended worship here on our first Sunday in Ghana.

The Derr Family with the brethren at the Amakon Church of Christ. Harold is taking the picture. Diana is holding little Jerry, Comfort's baby.

The Derr Family on our first Sunday in Ghana. Back row: Debbie, Harold and Jane Ann. Front row: Janice, Cathy, John and Diana.

September 9, 1963

Early the next morning, Comfort, B.O. Samuels' wife, and I went to Kumasi Central Market to buy vegetables. Comfort was dressed in a typical Ghanaian three-piece garment. A colorful floor length yellow, black and white piece of cloth was gracefully draped around her body forming a skirt. The blouse was fitted at the bodice with a scooped neckline and with a ruffle at the waistline. She carried her four-month-old son Jerry tied neatly to her back with a shawl. As the wife of B.O. Samuels, Harold's interpreter and fellow preacher, she was my helper trying to indoctrinate me into my new environment. Harold had driven us to the market while B.O. pointed the way. Harold and B.O. stayed behind to visit while Comfort and I completed the shopping.

Comfort and I got out of the car and I followed her across the street and down a narrow, muddy strip between two old buildings. As I looked up, I had my first glimpse of the renowned Kumasi Central Marketplace. Thousands of Ghanaians dotted nearly every square inch of the many acres of marketplace sprawling out before us. I looked around and I could not see any other white shoppers. Already the marketplace was humming with the excitement of thousands of people doing their daily shopping.

Comfort knew exactly where she was going. She confidently walked at a very rapid pace. As I turned my head to the right, I could see two vultures perched on the tin roof of one of the stands. Seller booths or stands consisted of posts holding up a tin roof for protection from the hot sun. The floor was red clay. The two women sellers inside the stand acted as if the vultures were a familiar sight. As I looked to the left, I could see an open sewer. On one end I could see a small child playing in the muddy water. On the other end I could see an older child urinating in the same sewer. I quickly turned to look for Comfort. She was far ahead of me. I hurried to catch up.

I found Comfort by the numerous rows of tables filled with plantain, yams, bananas, red peppers and cabbage. Comfort went to the banana table and palavered. This means she bargained for a good price from the woman seller. After the negotiation was over, Comfort said that the price was "too dear" which means it was too expensive. Then Comfort walked on. She would only buy items at a good price. At this point, I was willing to pay any price to leave, but she was walking too fast to stop her. The further we walked into the heart of the market, the more crowded and dirty it became. The ground beneath us was spongy, sticky, red mud with large crevices and ditches that we had to climb over. All the stands were very close together. We had a difficult time pushing our way from one stand to the next. Everyone was talking quite loudly. I couldn't understand a word.

Nearly all the stands were operated by Ghanaian women. Naked, undernourished children were running around crying. Some of the older women had no upper garments on. Some were nursing babies and trying to sell their vegetables at the same time. Garbage, filth and litter were strewn on our pathway. The hot African sun beat down producing pungent, unpleasant odors. I climbed over the ditches the best I could as Comfort was walking very fast and I was afraid of losing her. The ground beneath us was very muddy and slick. We had many uphill grades to climb and it took all my strength to keep from falling down.

We visited many vegetable and fruit stands and purchased lettuce, carrots, pineapple, bananas, plantain, yams and avocados. Next Comfort bought a big wicker basket and put all the produce in it and palavered for a boy to carry it for us on his head. When this was accomplished, we went to another part of the market where she stopped to buy her daily food. She purchased smoked dried fish, tomatoes and some native fruit. We then walked very quickly back to the car, pushing our way through the throng of people. It took about an hour to purchase the food we needed. *I prayed that God was walking through that market with me. I so needed His help.* This scene kept going through my mind when I got home. Oh, how God has blessed me and all the women in America to allow us the privilege of being born in America. We have the opportunity to choose to worship God and Jesus Christ, educational facilities to expand our knowledge and freedom to move about. How easy it is for us to go into an air conditioned supermarket and purchase all the food we need and a few of the luxuries that we find so essential. This was not true in Ghana. Most of the Ghanaian women worked in order to purchase enough food for their family to survive. Ghanaian women have many children, but this did not exempt them from the necessity of working away from home.

The job available to most women was selling in the local marketplace. An average seller made about twenty to twenty-five dollars a month. Her hours were from six o'clock in the morning until her merchandise is sold. Usually she would not be able to leave for home until late in the afternoon. Then she would take care of her household chores. It took about two hours for her to prepare a meal over a charcoal fire outside her one-room mud hut. Sometimes the food required hours of pounding with a long wooden stick. The daily washing was accomplished by bending over a bucket and rubbing the clothes until they were clean. The clothes were then laid on the ground to dry. Though much progress has been made in this new country since its independence to raise the standard of living and to lift the heavy burden placed on the Ghanaian women, nevertheless these conditions still exist today.

Thank you, God, for blessing me and please help me to make a difference in the lives of these people in Ghana.

Comfort and Jerry.

Jane Ann purchasing food at Kumasi Central Market.

Letter to my parents, Loran and Luetta Critchlow, in San Diego, California
September 10, 1963

Dear Mother and Daddy,

We arrived safely Saturday evening around 8:00 P.M. So much has happened in the last few days that I hardly know where to begin. We left Philadelphia Airport about 4:00 P.M. Wendell and Betty Broom, Jean and Jerry Reynolds, Katie Hynes and Grandma and Granddad Derr went to the airport to tell us goodbye. The ladies at Cedars Church of Christ presented me with a beautiful white orchid and Harold a buttoner. Jerry Reynolds led us in a prayer. Final good-byes were said and we boarded the plane, a National Airlines Plane, making a short run to New York Idlewild Airport. We were sure a sight getting on the plane. We had eleven suitcases, seven flight bags, a camera bag, and portable radio. Surprisingly, we were still a few pounds under our limit. We had about a two hour layover in New York before we boarded a Pan-Am DC8 Jet on an eight hour flight direct to Ghana. We were delayed an hour at Idlewild because twenty planes were ahead of us in the flight pattern.

Once on the jet, we had seats in the back of the plane all together near a large group of Peace Corps workers bound for Dakar and Accra. We had mostly a smooth flight over except for a few rough spots. Flying over the ocean is much rougher than flying over land. Watching the beautiful sun rise at 40,000 feet above the clouds was a fascinating sight. We got off the plane at Dakar so they could clean the plane. Our next stop was Roberts Field in Monrovia. Circling the field getting ready to land, we could see the primitive extremely thick bush, lots of winding rivers, and swampy land. We could see quite well the primitive villages. Our brief stop in Monrovia ended before we could really comprehend that we were a long way from home. We boarded the plane again and in a couple of hours we were in Accra. However, we had to wait in Accra six hours for another plane to take us to Kumasi.

The Davenports and many Ghanaian brethren had waited to meet us. We headed to the Davenports to eat, and then we traveled to our new home. As soon as we arrived at our new home, we hurriedly unpacked our suitcases, made up our beds, and fell into bed exhausted. We had not slept the night before.

I'll write more soon. We arrived safely. Write soon.

Love,
Jane Ann

September 10, 1963
I wrote in my journal

On the third night in Ghana, after the girls were all bedded down for the night, I propped myself up in bed. Harold and John were out in one of the faraway villages preaching. John always insisted on going everywhere his Daddy went so tonight Harold, B.O. Samuels, his interpreter, Dwayne Davenport, and John left on their venture after an early supper. I opened up my daily journal to write.

Now comes the time of reflection. I am beginning to realize how precious my time is and how I have wasted so much of it in the past concentrating on complaining, what others think, what to wear, criticizing others, and other nonproductive activities.

The people here live a very simple but difficult life, however, they don't complain. They sing, dance, and play the drums and other musical instruments as they work. They take time to visit with the people they meet at the village square. Women visit as they wash their clothes at a nearby stream. They take the time to enjoy the now. I have so much to learn.

We must meet our challenges head on and pray that God will show us the way. Our challenges now are: getting the children enrolled in school; getting our house cleaned with fresh paint, tile on the floor, beds for all the children and an open closet rack to store our clothes and protect them from mold. *Dear God, help me with an extra degree of patience. I really need your help.*

One evening at the end of our first week in Ghana, our family sat around a large rectangular dinner table. We had to really stretch our arms to hold hands as we said our prayer. After our prayer ended I looked around the table.

"Mommy, I miss our round oak table in America." Janice reflected.

"Don't you remember?" Debbie giggled, "It was so crowded. Our elbows touched because Mommy and Cathy were left-handed and the rest of us were right-handed."

"Daddy would always tease us." Diana added.

"Remember when I spilled milk?" John laughed.

"Then at the end of the meal we would argue about whose turn it was to do the dishes." Diana remarked with an impish grin.

"Now Comfort does the dishes," Debbie giggled.

"Hopefully tomorrow we can get you children enrolled in school." Harold replied as he leaned back in his chair. His voice was seriously clear.

The laughter died down as Janice added, "Daddy, that's all right. We can go to the library and bring home books to read. I noticed a large library not far from here."

Harold opened his mouth to reply, and then closed it. Suddenly a loud knock on the door interrupted our family mealtime and Harold walked over to open the door. It was John Law, our nightwatch. He said that he had just killed a large snake in the open sewer in the backyard.

I don't know if I can ever cope with snakes outside and lizards inside. When I'm in bed at night, I can hear the lizards rustling and scrambling over the wooden cornices at the top of the drapes. However, the sound of the rain hitting the tin roof and the rhythm of the drums from the neighboring village seems to sooth my tensions and put me to sleep.

One of our big battles was the struggle to communicate. Even though English was the official language, it was only used in government and business circles in the cities and urban areas. Akan in its various dialects enjoys a wide usage throughout the country. It was a trade language for most Ghanaians. About nine languages were used in the Ghanaian school system. Most Ghanaians spoke more languages than their own. There were about 60 language groups in Ghana and John Law was from the North and he speaks a different language. (Boateng)

A few days later while everyone was asleep, I sat on the couch in the living room with a lantern for light and put my racing thoughts on paper. I could hear the frogs, the crickets, the talking drums outside and inside I could hear someone snoring.

September 15, 1963
I wrote in my journal

I am so happy that the landlord is going to let us paint and clean up the dirty concrete floors with fresh new tile. My mind started to wander. I smiled as I remembered that special day in May 1963 half a world away in Terre Haute, Indiana, when God helped us to sell our three bedroom home with plenty of roaming space and we purchased a 17 foot travel trailer to live in while we were raising funds for our Ghanaian venture. We had to buy a heavy duty trailer hitch for the International Harvester Travel All for our trip. The big day came. The trailer was delivered.

We all stood a long time admiring our new home. Our 17 foot trailer was silver on the outside trimmed in turquoise. We walked up two steps at the door on the side and as we went inside looking to the right was an oblong shaped dining table with a white Formica top. Light brown upholstered seats were perched on each side of the table. The table would drop down and make a bed at night.

Looking up at the overhang was a large king-size bed. Looking to the left was a galley kitchen. Lined up on one side of the hallway was the sink with a small refrigerator under the counter. On the opposite side were the furnace, hot water heater and stove. Further down, the wall jutted out to make room for a small bathroom with a toilet and shower. At the very end of the trailer was a couch that made a double bed at night. All the walls were light pine paneling and pretty beige and brown café-type curtains covered all the large louvered windows. We discovered a tiny closet by the refrigerator. Standing at the bathroom door looking down the kitchen galley hallway and hanging high on the left wall was a round kerosene lamp which provided light at night for the entire trailer. The floor was covered with dark brown tweed indoor/outdoor carpet.

After closely studying the situation, Debbie questioned, "Daddy, how do we all fit into that small space?"

"We can eat in shifts or find a roadside picnic table. It will be a lot of fun and just like a long camping trip. Debbie, Diana and Janice can sleep in the king-size bed over the table. Mom and Cathy can sleep on the couch bed in the back and John and I can sleep on the bed made from the table or if John gets tired of my snoring, he can sleep on an air mattress on the floor." Harold answered in a very matter of fact voice.

I remember reassuring the children that we would be just fine. It was quite an exciting adventure living in the trailer for four and a half months, traveling over 5,000 miles from Indiana to California and then crisscrossing the country and ending up in Wilmington, Delaware.

One big problem was lack of privacy. Eleven-year-old Debbie asked for her own private drawer. When I told her we didn't have any, she found a storage space at the end of the couch where we slept. This was a very important issue for an eleven-year-old.

The trailer was very hot because we had to keep the louvered windows closed during the day while we drove. Then at night, we had to wait several hours for the trailer to air out and to lower the temperature somewhat.

Water was very scarce so we could take showers only at camp sites. A tiny closet was on one side of the refrigerator. We kept an iron on the top shelf and used the tabletop as our ironing board. The table wasn't big enough for all of us to eat at once so we would try to find a roadside park with tables. For breakfast, we would eat in shifts or eat in the car while driving.

Now thinking about our life in Ghana, this house seems spacious. It is hot but a breeze usually circulates the air. Suddenly my thoughts drifted in a different direction and I wondered if the fundraising commitments would materialize. My thoughts shut down and I decided to go to bed.

Our Fundraising Map

We lived in the trailer 109 days from May 21, 1963 to September 6, 1963 as we zigzagged across the United States. The International Harvester Travel All served us well with no major breakdowns except some flat tires. We travel 5,724 miles.

Harold standing in front of the International Harvester Travel All that pulled our travel trailer. This picture was taken in the parking lot of the Palmdale, California Church of Christ.

September 24, 1963

Hello Everyone!

We've been in Ghana seventeen days. Everything here is a problem. In order to buy groceries, you must go all over town to complete your grocery list. A store will have only a couple of items on your list. Then the merchandise comes from countries that the US doesn't trade with and the names are all strange. Vegetables are called by different names here. Kraft Mayonnaise sells for one dollar a pint; ground beef from Denmark is one dollar a pound. We do get wonderful whole wheat bread for 14 cents. We have a large garden started all ready. The plants are about three inches and we are looking forward to eating what we have planted: tomatoes, lettuce,

Brussels sprouts, Savoy (which I thought was cabbage but it isn't), cucumbers, cauliflower, onions, green beans and corn. Our night watch, John Law, also our gardener, is taking really good care of our garden. He is very knowledgeable although he does not speak English or Twi. We make signs. We have a lovely front yard with lots of beautiful flowers, cannas, marigolds, snapdragons, orchid trees, cactus, and flowers I've never seen. John Law cuts the grass with a long wide knife by hand and also planted the seeds with the same instrument. He carries water for the garden, covers it up with giant leaves, picks all the dead flowers everyday and does any other heavy job we have. He is a very big strong man. Most of the Ghanaians from this area are very short small men and everyone really jumps when a big man says something. He is a good night watch. Harold gets good prices and good work done, too.

John Law is our night watch, gardener, handyman and friend.

The house here was very dirty. We were quite pleased when the landlord said that we could paint it inside and outside, lay tile throughout the house and take it out of the rent money. The painter started work today in the kitchen. It will probably take us two or three months to finish. The house had very little furniture. So we are buying some furniture. Right now the carpenter is making us beds. We need two. You don't buy something here and say, deliver it tomorrow. First, the carpenter meets with you to discuss what you want, and then you bargain for a price. After that he starts to work and finishes it in about a week if you are fortunate. Finally you hire a lorry to bring it home. The carpenter makes only one item at a time, so it takes considerable time to get anything.

Our house in Kumasi is on the left. The preaching students lived in the unfinished house on the right where classes were also conducted.

The house had a large front porch with six concrete pillars and pipe banisters. Although four to six doors graced the front porch, we used only one door. As you walked into the house, you entered a large living room / dining room area. The room had white walls and a grey tile floor. A light wood, frame sofa and two chairs were in the living room. The sofa and chairs were topped with blue kapok pillows covered in a plastic product. The pillows leaked when someone sat on the sofa or chairs and scattered kapok on the floor.

The master bedroom on the right boasted two sets of double crank-type windows on each side of the room. A king-size bed was on the right and a desk and an old tube-type ham radio were on the left. The right corner of the bed was up against two sets of double windows. Later on, John Law made us open air closets because in a closed closet the clothes would mildew.

The living room / dining room was open. In the middle of the room a door opening led to a long hallway where a wing jetted out. To the right was John and Cathy's bedroom. In the middle of the hall were two doors. Behind one door was the toilet room. A shower and a small sink were behind the other door. The walls of these small rooms were covered with red and grey tile. To the left was another bedroom used by Diana and Janice. Their bed headboard was against the wall facing the hall and their feet were near the double windows.

A door at the end of the dining room led to a hallway. To the right end of the hallway was an outside door. On the left side of the hallway was a door leading to a small room called a maid's quarters. This was Debbie's room because it gave her the privacy she needed.

As you entered the hallway from the dining room, directly to the left was the kitchen. The floor was red and white tile. In the far left corner was a small stove with a propane gas tank. On the right side along the wall, was a long shelf with a sink set up to wash and drain vegetables as well as dishes.

A baptistery was outside the house in the back yard. The yard had open sewers. The house had a tin roof that produced strange, soothing sounds as rain beat on it at night. The house had many windows that allowed lightning to light up the entire house at night.

Behind the house was a small building with three offices: storage room, Bible Correspondence Office, and a school room in the garage.

After six trips of negotiating, we were able to enroll our children in school. No one here is in a hurry! As it stands now, John and Cathy will both be enrolled in the first grade of the British School and will begin in about two weeks. Debbie started Monday. She is in Secondary School Form 1 at Kwame Nkrumah Technology School which is on the campus of the University. This is equivalent to the seventh grade in America. Of the 21 boys and 6 girls, she is the only white person in her class. Janice will go to the British School in November and Diana will go to the same school in December.

Debbie could not go because they do not accept children 12 years old or older. All of the British children 12 years old or older go back to England for school and the American children all are home schooled using the Calvert Correspondence Courses. We are going to see if Debbie does well in the University School before we order the home school courses.

Recently we held our first Vacation Bible School in the Bible Training School compound. We had five classes with fourteen teachers. Our total enrollment was over 300. Our average attendance was 197 each day. This was a joint effort with Dwayne and Jane Davenport. Three classes met in small classrooms about 9 by 12. One class of pre-school children averaged 98 in attendance and met outside with no shade. One other class met in the Amakon church building. We had no discipline problems here compared to America. Probably the reason is because the custom here is for an adult who sees a child misbehaving to correct that child with whatever measure he thinks appropriate regardless of whose child it is. These Ghanaian children respect any adult and this makes it much easier to work with them. In one of the classes a boy about 12 years old misbehaved and the teacher sent him home. In a short time the boy came back to publicly apologize to the teachers, the school and the students, beg forgiveness and asked to come back. He came every day. Even the pre-school children came with their baby brothers and sisters tied to their backs. One little boy who came every day, had to crawl as his hips and legs were so tiny. He was about 8 years old. He walked on his knees and got around very well. He always had the sweetest smile. Some of the older children were nearly blind with cataracts on their eyes. A lot of the children were from Muslim backgrounds. As a direct result of our Vacation Bible School, one of our Ghanaian preachers started a weekly Saturday morning Bible Class. The children asked us to hold this class.

Love,
Jane Ann

One evening after being in Ghana for twenty-five days, I propped myself up in bed. Harold and John were out preaching again and the girls were all in their rooms reading. We had gone to the library the previous day and brought home seventeen books. The girls were thrilled and could hardly wait until they could start reading.

I picked up my journal to write. The words just didn't seem to come. One chilling thought kept going around and around in my head like an engine out of control: Will we be able to raise sufficient funds to carry on the work here?

We launched out in faith, arriving here without funds for our return passage and without sufficient monthly support. After we got here we discovered that we had no transportation and now Dwayne has announced that he doubts if anyone will be found to replace them when they return to America in June. What shall we do? We inherited a large size financial mess. How can we do this work without help? *I'm in a quandary, and I don't understand, God. You showed us that You wanted us here but the financial support has been scarce and the needs here are so tremendous. No one can solve this crisis except You, God. Where are You now? We need You so.*

For days a thought kept trickling into my mind and I kept trying to block it out: Would Daddy be willing to contact churches around Southern California and present the financial needs in Ghana?

In the past, I have had an on again off again relationship with Daddy stemming from painful childhood memories. I try to forgive him, but sometimes it doesn't seem to work out that way. As a child I saw him as very handsome, always well-dressed, and full of vitality and a high achiever at work. With only an eighth grade education, he had worked his way up the ladder to General Manager of the largest bakery in Terre Haute. He had a God-given talent of getting along with people, which helped him to excel in the challenging environment of managing seventy-five employees.

However at home, Daddy was a different person. Sadly, he always fought close personal relationships and became angry. Grief over the loss of parents, his little sister, Ella Mae, and a rebellious younger brother had left deep wounds. The pain seemed to be the hardest when he was confronted in a family situation. My perception as an adult viewed him as being a very complex person who had not known how to process his grief. However, at times, he was a very caring person at home. When I was thirteen, he bought me my first corsage. I was so proud.

If God, the Bible, or church were mentioned, our home became a battle zone. I remember Mother pleading with Daddy to go to church with us, but he always became extremely angry and Mother invariably would end up in tears. Sadly, Mother was usually the one who received the brunt of his wrath. Mother was a beautiful woman with short, jet black, curly hair, with an ivory complexion, big black sparkling eyes and the warmest smile that framed her radiant face. She didn't deserve his anger.

Whenever we had asked Mother about Daddy's anger, she gave us a firm, long and loving hug that assured us that everything would work out just fine. She said, "We'll pray about that."

Daddy had worked extended hours, and then came home and drank his sorrows away. His two to three packs of Camels a day did nothing to quell his uncontrollable temper. I could still hear my Mother screaming, "No! No!" after Daddy came home one night and ripped Mother's new red long-sleeved blouse with the gold buttons to shreds. I never did understand why.

I remembered all the times Mother took my brother Jack, Ruby, Daddy's younger sister that lived with us, and me to church—no small effort on her part. We rode the bus transferring several times along the way. At the final stop, we walked to the small white frame church building in the northern part of town and entered via a little front porch. Mother never complained. She instead turned her concerns over to God. Many times I had seen her in the front porch swing reading her Bible with the tattered front cover and underlining her favorite passages. One she always quoted to me was, "Your Word I have hidden in my heart that I might not sin against You." (Psalms 119:11) Mother's greatest joy in life had been teaching her second grade Bible class.

Often at night I had hidden a flashlight under my pillow so I could read my Bible before going to sleep. My dream had been to marry a preacher, and while I was the least likely candidate, I prayed earnestly that God would send a preacher my way.

When I was ten years old, I had decided I wanted to be baptized. For some reason, all baptisms were at night; I think it was because it took a long time to prepare the baptistery. Buses didn't run after dark so Daddy agreed to drive us to church. He refused to go inside the church. Instead he waited in the cold gray Plymouth for us to return.

Just a short time before Harold and I were married, Daddy turned his life around. He had been baptized and immediately stopped his 2 to 3 packs of Camels-a-day-habit, and greatly controlled his temper—most of the time. Mother had beamed every time we talked about Daddy's decision to turn his life over to God. She reminded me of the power of prayer. Daddy then became a dynamic soul winner, teaching many people in home Bible studies the grace and mercy of Jesus Christ and the power of forgiveness in our lives. Daddy's years of rebellion to the Word of God spurred him on to be a greater and a more useful servant of Christ. He deeply understood the bondage and fear of a life outside of Christ. After moving to San Diego, Daddy had found many opportunities to help young men and women stationed at the Naval Facility nearby showing them the Jule Miller Bible Filmstrips and had baptized over 65.

Bringing my thoughts back to our current dilemma, I decided that God was prodding me to ask Daddy to go on the fund raising trail. *I prayed and asked God to help me to have a forgiving heart. Then I wrote in my journal all of the bad feelings that I had been harboring about Daddy. Next I prayed that God would release me from that bondage and lift my bad feelings one step at a time and to replace these poisonous feelings with love—God's love.*

The next day Harold and I drafted a letter to Daddy asking for his help.

September 25, 1963

Dear Grandma and Grandpa Critchlow,

We are in Ghana now. I just love the people here. They are so friendly. When you come home from church they all wave to you and say come back.

We are having VBS now. I teach the first and second grade. Debbie teaches the pre-school. Have you had your VBS yet?

Debbie might start to school next week. Cathy and John will start the last part of October and Janice in November. I won't start until after Christmas. So we have a long time to wait.

We don't have our barrels yet. We hope to have them soon.

We have so many letters to write. So don't be upset if this is a short letter. Daddy said he had a long list of letters for us to write to church classes.

I will write soon. Bye.

Love,
Diana

October 1, 1963

Dear Mother and Daddy,

We received your letter last night. Daddy, thank you for being willing to go on the fund raising venture to help us, and to follow up on our support. As we told you earlier, Jerry Reynolds' old microbus with 100,000 miles on it died on their way to the airport going home. We tried to have it repaired, but we couldn't get parts and also it was too costly. In addition, we need to raise money for our return trip to America. Thank you again. God bless.

Our barrels are still not here. We have many things to do so I'll make this short and write more later. Everything is a problem here.

Love,
Jane Ann

October 14, 1963

When the letter from my parents came on October 14, we decided to read it to all the children at the same time at the dinner table.

"Grandma and Grandpa Critchlow want to know what you children would like to have as a Christmas present," Harold questioned as he studied the wide-eyed faces.

"Remember, Grandma works in a toy store." Harold added.

"Daddy, I miss Ginger." blurted out John.

"Don't you know we can't bring a dog here?" rationalized Diana.

"Why can't we bring Ginger here?" questioned Janice.

"I don't know," replied Harold scratching his head." but I'll find out." he added.

"Daddy, if we bring her here it will be a little bit like home. She's family." Debbie smiled, as though surprised at the thought.

Cathy looked up for the first time. She seemed to be picturing in her mind days of playing with Ginger. "Daddy, could we give Ginger iced tea like Grandma Derr does?" Cathy questioned with an impish smile. "She would be a good watch dog." she added.

At the end of the entire discussion, we prayed to find a way to bring Ginger, our Boxer pup to Ghana for Christmas.

October 15, 1963

Dear Mother and Daddy,

We received your letter last night. We have talked it over and the Christmas gift our entire family would appreciate more than any other gift would be to bring Ginger, our dog over here. The Derr's are taking good care of her and even gave her iced tea. We miss her terribly and she would be an excellent watch dog!

We are going to ask the Derr's the same thing. Deposit what you intend to spend on Christmas into our Delaware bank account and tell Craig Henry what it is for and he will take care of it. We will need American currency to pay for shipping Ginger.

We are having a four-day gospel meeting this week in the market-place in Amakon. The brethren from Amakon brought benches from the church building and two Tilley lamps. Dwayne Davenport drove his microbus with the loud speakers. Dwayne and Harold both preached and used B.O. Samuel as the interpreter. We had a lot of people enroll in our Bible Correspondence Courses and 300 to 350 attended each night. We did not have enough benches for everyone and many stood for nearly two hours to hear the sweet story of Jesus and how much he loved them. It was unbelievable! This is so different than America where very few people take the time to listen. We are going to start taking Twi lessons soon. Write us.

Love,
Jane Ann

Late October, 1963

When our barrels finally arrived from America, I could hardly wait to open them. It had been so long since we packed the barrels, and so many events had taken place that I couldn't remember what to expect to see in the barrels. The truck finally arrived at the house bringing the barrels from the dock. We all had so much fun discovering our treasures from America: sheets, pillowcases, towels, dishes, table linens, kitchen utensils, toys, clothes, 315 books, sewing items, electrical tools, drafting tools, carpenter tools, engineer tools, mechanic tools, office supplies, violin, balloons, bubblegum, bath items, make-up, curlers, clothes hangers, gift wrapping paper, Christmas tree ornaments, canned and powdered milk, vitamins, various non-prescription medicines, first aid supplies to treat Ghanaians, missionary equipment catalog, physicians catalog, and Bible class material. When I found the books, I quickly set aside several of my past daily journals to read later.

Later than night when everyone was asleep, I loaded some of the books under my arm and went to the living room couch to read. I picked up one of the journals, and opened to an entry marked Barstow, California, June 16, 1963 written on our fundraising venture.

"This is Sunday morning. We got up early and went to worship services. The preacher Brother Cooper is leaving and the eldership has been dissolved. Everyone seemed to be so disgruntled, unhappy and very unfriendly. They did not want us to come, but they had failed to write or call to let us know. So after driving 115 miles to get to Barstow, we received a very cold reception.

Tears came to my eyes remembering the old days when we were warmly received with open arms. I thought of all the times we had driven from Boron after worship services on Sunday mornings to baptize someone in the Barstow baptistery. I thought of the times that Harold had stood in that pulpit and had been encouraged so much by their kind words. *Why? God, are You still listening to our prayers? Where are You?*

After services, three young couples noticed that we were lingering around. We didn't have much food left. We had all shared a can of peaches for breakfast and our stomachs were now growling. We only had $6.82 in our pocket to feed seven people. *What shall we do? God please help us!*

One of the young couples came over to speak to us. They invited us to go with them on a picnic. *Thank You God!* During the conversations that followed, they inquired about our mission plans, and asked how things were going. We explained our present predicament. Without any warning, they got together and decided to give us $46. *Thank You God!*

We decided to drive on to Palmdale for evening services. Afterward, Lester and June Nichols invited us over for supper. We had a lovely meal of ham and salads. With full stomachs that night, we parked the trailer in the church parking lot to spend the night."

Notes from my journal, June 17, 1963 to June 20, 1963

"The next morning, we got up early, packed a picnic lunch and drove to Tehachapi Mountain Park. We roasted wieners. It was so beautiful, restful and cool. We had just left 100 degree temperatures in the desert. I took a book that Mother had purchased for me entitled, "Woman to Woman" by Eugenia Price, and found a shady place to read. Harold and the children went hiking. Toward evening, we drove back to Palmdale and had an enjoyable visit with the Burke Family. We parked our trailer in the Palmdale church parking lot again. Before bedtime, we decided to go back to Tehachapi in the morning.

Early the next morning, we packed our lunch and drove to Tehachapi Mountain Park. We enjoy the mountains so much. I went off again, found a beautiful spot and read while Harold and the children hiked and played baseball together. In the evening we all watched the sunset together and then had our daily family devotional. We sang and sang until we were hoarse, then we drove to Palmdale after dark.

It was now Wednesday, I had straightened the trailer, and then I had taken the washing and the book that Mother had bought me to a laundry mat. A sweet lady, Joyce Tate, stopped me at the laundry mat and talked to me at great length about the book I was reading. She told me about her prayer group and explained how they exchanged Christian books. When I told her that we were going to Ghana, she said she would mail me books. She then immediately went home and brought back three books for me to keep. One of them was called, "The Christian's Secret of a Happy Life", by Hannah Whitsall Smith.

In the evening we went to the Lancaster church where Harold was scheduled to speak. Before we arrived, the men had decided not to help us; however, several individuals gave us $18. Then a good brother Marian Owens asked Harold how we were doing and Harold said we had $3.87. The men met again and gave us $300. Brother Owens will send us $100 in July. We were so thrilled. *Thank You, God!* We then drove back to Palmdale where the trailer was parked."

Reading this journal jarred me back to our life now in Ghana. *Thank You God for reminding me of Your loving care and concern for us.* I closed the journal and went to bed.

November 3, 1963

Dear Mother and Daddy,

Don't be disturbed if I don't write quite so often. We are so busy. This is a very demanding work. I have lots of bookkeeping to do. We must report to Cedars all the money spent for the working fund. Everything is in shillings and pence. So I must convert it into American currency. Yes, as you know, I haven't had any college courses in accounting. In addition, to make it more difficult I have no calculator or adding machine. The deadlines for reports are extremely critical so people will continue our support.

In addition, Harold and I must get the written report on the work out on time. We both discuss, make notes, then I must type it up. We are also trying to publish a paper for the Ghana brethren.

The dry season is coming on now and it is so hot in the afternoons. Ghana is so near the equator and the noon day sun is almost overhead throughout the year. April to September is the rainy season and there are two dry periods with the driest period in December, January and February. In the dry season it rains only at night and then not every night.

We have been getting up at 5A.M. to get everything done so we have been going to bed around 9P.M. or earlier. The early start really increases our energy level. We have so much to do and so few to do it. We are all in good health and eating very nourishing meals although it takes most of our $500 a month salary for food. The cost of living went up over ten percent the last few weeks. We are managing though and we are thankful that our entire salary has been assured from one church, Cedars in Wilmington, Delaware.

The children are still happy with their schools and Debbie told us today that her Polish girl friend is going home to Poland next month. Debbie will miss her very much. Now Debbie will be the only white person in her class.

We still do not have a car. The microbus money is coming in very slowly. However, if we had the money, we still could not buy one. There are no cars for sale here. We must wait for one to be imported. We were promised a car in December. We have been borrowing Davenport's car which is a hardship on them.

I mailed you a package last week. Let me know when you receive it.

Love,
Jane Ann

November 8, 1963
Letter to Harold's Parents Tonie and Susie Derr
Terre Haute, Indiana

Dear Mom and Dad,

We just received your letter. Thanks for all the facts that you have gathered concerning Ginger. We are all very grateful. Since John can't go to school, he is constantly begging for a dog. He is having a much more difficult time adjusting than the other children. Last night he wanted us to send him back to see mam maw.

Since it is going to cost more than we expected to send Ginger here, would you please work with Mother and Daddy and put together the money you were going to spend for Christmas? We will make up the difference. The children really miss Ginger. I know that you must feel that we are very foolish. However, there are so many things the children do not have here. They never complain except they miss Ginger so very much.

Harold loves the work here although we all have much to do. In fact, it is so much that we feel we are always behind. The need here is so great. It is so thrilling to see how God's Word can transform even an idol worshipper into a child of God and a believer that Jesus Christ is the Son of God. One of our preachers even bore the name of a pagan idol until he came in touch with the Word of God. He accepted Christianity and changed his name to Emmanuel, "God with us".

Paganism is so steeped in fear. Fear of witchcraft is intense. Ancestral worship is common and sacrifices are made to pacify these spirits so they won't come back and do harm to the family. Harold and I are searching for books about the history, culture, art and religion of the Ghanaian to help us to better understand and communicate with them.

Our entire family started taking Twi lessons. An instructor comes to our house three days a week and teaches us for one hour. It is very interesting. The children are all excited about the classes. The instructor said the children will learn faster than we will. It is a tonal language and I find it very difficult. However, this is a necessity as you rarely find anyone in the bush who can speak English. It is so important for us to know Twi because so many sick people come to us wanting medicine. We usually give the sick aspirin or "Maalox". Our medical trunk got lost but it came Saturday.

Getting back to Ginger, when we come back to the States, we plan to come via freighter and it won't cost any extra to bring Ginger home. The Broom's told us that this is a good way to travel. You are allowed a sizable amount of baggage per person. However the drawback, you must reserve space nine months in advance. It would take about five to six weeks to come home. This sounds good because we are not looking forward to flying after our Ghana Airways flight. That really shook us up.

Must close and get back to work. Write soon.

Love,
Jane Ann

November 9, 1963

Dear Mother and Daddy,

We just received your letter yesterday. We are so glad everything is going so well for you.

This week we had a group of the Ghanaian brethren over for lunch. They came to clear off the land behind us. The Ghana Government gave the church five acres of land to build a church building, the Ghana Bible Training School and two missionary houses. We have cleared off about half of the boundary line. Part of this land is quite low and a breeding place for mosquitoes and snakes. We thank God only one snake got in our way. One of the men killed it before it bit anyone.

I had Comfort prepare the food for the workers at her home and bring it over. We served 12 of them at our dining room table just like I would in America with napkins, tablecloth, silverware, and iced water. What a shock! First, the napkins disappeared. Next only a few liked the ice. They eat with their hands and no silverware. It was interesting to watch. We wanted them to be at ease and very comfortable. They were! Food was all over the floor! They stood up to eat part of the time. No passing of food. They just grabbed food while walking around the table. They did enjoy the meal and consumed a lot of food.

Harold laughed at me for using napkins. He said he observed them as they tucked away the napkins to use later as toilet paper! The other missionaries have even charged a few pence for little Bible tracts because if you don't, the people will probably take them home to use as toilet paper. The toilet paper here has a texture of thin, stiff wax paper.

The children are getting some very valuable exposure to children from other countries. Last week Diana and Janice were invited to spend the day with a girl in their class from Ceylon. The girls had some interesting stories to tell. They enjoyed the food very much. It was served in many courses with very fancy linens and dishes. They burned incense. The mother had a red mark on her forehead.

Last night Debbie had the Polish girl from her school over to spend the night. She is a very sweet girl but very bashful. She and her father are here alone and the mother is still in Poland. Their home is 100 miles outside of Warsaw. She has a boxer in Poland. She speaks very little English but we still had a great visit and friendly hugs are an international language.

The children can't wait to see Ginger. They even preferred to have Ginger here than to each have a new bike. Write soon.

Love,
Jane Ann

November 12, 1963

When we took the children to the library today, I decided to find some books about Ghana. I found a very interesting book about the geography and the people.

Geography

Ghana is located in West Africa near the equator. It is bordered on the north by Upper Volta, on the east by Togo, on the south by the Atlantic Ocean, and on the west by Ivory Coast. Ghana covers approximately 92,100 square miles and its capital city is Accra. Ghana is slightly smaller than the State of Oregon. The terrain is composed mainly of rain forest and savanna. Ghana has a tropical climate.

Since Ghana is only a few degrees north of the equator, the only seasonal changes are distinct wet and dry seasons. The noon day sun is almost overhead throughout the year. The best time to visit is during the December—February dry season, when day temperatures are in the 80'sF and 90'sF and the nights are in the 70'sF. Another dry season occurs in July and August, but it is much hotter. The worse time to visit is April—June, when it's the rainiest. The rainfall is up to 86 inches per year. A dry northeast wind known as the harmattan blows almost continuously in January and February. The eastern coastal belt is warm and comparatively dry; the southwest corner has the highest humidity and rainfall, while the north is frequently hot and dry.

Line squalls or tornados occur mostly at the beginning and ending of the rainy season and are most frequently found in parts of Ashanti.

Ghana's natural resources are: gold, timber, industrial diamonds, bauxite, manganese, fish, rubber, hydropower, petroleum, silver, salt and limestone.

Cocoa

Cocoa was first grown successfully in Mampong, Ghana in the forest of Akwapim. Since World War 1, cocoa has been the main source of Ghana's wealth. Kumasi became one of the chief centers for cocoa farming and in the 1960's Ashanti took first place in cocoa production.

The Oil Palm

The oil palms grow wild in most parts of the forest. Palm oil is one of the chief fats of the world used for cooking or sometimes margarine or soup.

Timber

The Ghana forest is rich in a variety of trees such as mahogany, wawa, sopele, coffee, rubber, bananas, and others. Timber is second only to cocoa in exports.

Fishing in Sea and Rivers

At least 100 fishing villages cover the 334 miles of coastline. The average distance between villages is only three miles. In every single town and village on the coast fishing is an important industry. Rows of dugout canoes line up on the sandy shore and the drying nets are a familiar sight in every village and town. Nets are used to catch the fish: shark, tuna, and afafa. Men and boys spear fish in the lagoons. In times of low water, women pick clams from the river beds and transplant them to clam farms.

Mining and Minerals

The mines of Ghana are, next to cocoa the chief sources of the country's exports: gold, diamonds, manganese ore, and bauxite. One mine at Obuasi was described as the richest large gold mine in the world. In 33 years it had yielded five million fine ounces of gold: one ounce of gold from every ton of ore mined. Diamonds were first found in Ghana in 1919 in the gravel of the river Birim at Abomaso in Akim Abuakwa. Ghana exports more rough diamonds than any other country in the world except the Congo. Most of the salt in Ghana comes from the salt water lagoons in the eastern part of the coast.

Animals

Oribi, antelope, gazelle, lions, hyenas and crocodiles inhabit the rocks and shallows of the Volta and other rivers. Snakes abound, among them are black mamba, puff-adder, horned cerates and water snakes. A python too will often steal a goat. Lizards of many kinds abound everywhere. Hunters have almost destroyed some species of wild animals; however goats, pigs and poultry can be seen in every village. (Adams 1960) (Ghana at a Glance 1963) (Ghana Year Book 1964)

November 18, 1963

Dear Mother and Daddy,

We enjoyed getting your letter today and to learn why the first letters we received from family took so long to get here: they all went surface by boat. Thank God for air letters.

The Ghana Bible Training School will graduate the first class of preachers who have completed two years in the school. After the ceremony the preachers are going to sing, "I Know the Lord Will Find a Way for Me." That was the first song we taught them and it could be translated into Twi. Only a few songs can be translated into Twi because the language of the Ashanti is a tonal language.

We are planning a party for the graduates. We plan to serve cake and cokes and play a few games. The official game here is called Wari. This ancient game is played by two players using a Wari Board. This is a board hollowed out of wood into two parallel rows of six cups and with 48 pebbles. It is a very complicated game as each player circulates the pebbles across the board in two territories. We plan to bring back a Wari board.

We went to our first Ghanaian funeral a few days ago. The deceased was wealthy. For about a week, the relatives of the deceased stay home to receive callers. The dead are usually buried immediately or the next day. Afterward, the bed of the deceased is decorated very fancy in white. Next the relatives tell you where the body is laid in state. We went into the house. A large group of family was sitting in the living room. We made the rounds, shaking everyone's hand. We were then ushered to a seat. They asked us our mission. They said that our spokesman had told them that we had heard that someone had died. The spokesman for the family of the deceased said that was correct. He then told us how the death occurred. Next we were served orange soda pop. We drank it and then paid them a token of our sympathy. The few coins more than covered the cost of the orange soda pop. Then they came around and shook our hands and gave us permission to leave. We are buying books now to try to understand these customs.

The dry season is here and it has really zapped our energy. Write soon!

Love,
Jane Ann

Late November 1963
I wrote in my journal

Sunday night after Ghana Bible College Graduation, we came home exhausted. It was five hours long and Janice had a malaria attack during the ceremony. She was burning up with fever. The car was very hot so she came back to the graduation ceremony, stretched out on a long wooden bench by me and rested her head in my lap. We couldn't wait to get her home.

It was a beautiful ceremony and when they sang, "I Know the Lord will Find a Way for Me", my memory turned backward to another hot day July 21, 1963 in Snyder, Texas. We were on our fund raising trip headed back to Wilmington, Delaware. It had been a very discouraging trip. When we arrived at the Eastside Church of Christ in Snyder, we decided to try one more time to present the Ghana work. This congregation had a very large attractive building. Buford and Dorothy Browning met us. Buford was one of the elders and immediately arranged for Harold to present the Ghana work that night. After a very delicious chicken dinner at a nearby charming restaurant, we were able to enjoy a great fellowship with the Browning family. Later we went to the evening church service. It had been plainly announced that morning, so a large number of people attended.

While Harold was enthusiastically presenting the Ghana challenge and making the plea for help, John got his forearm stuck past his elbow, in the wooden opera seat. Since we were sitting two rows from the front, all eyes were on John's struggle to get free! I finally stood up and two men nearby observing the situation also stood up and helped me get John out of this predicament. While all of this confusion was developing, with unemotional calm, Harold made his plea for help. Harold used this ruckus to allow his great sense of humor to emerge.

Afterward, all seven of us took a long deep breath, walked up to the front of the audience and sang, "Kum Bah Yah", and "I Know the Lord will Find a Way for Me." After the service we were pleasantly surprised to discover that they had given us over $250. Buford Browning said it contained 80 one dollar bills, indicating that nearly everyone gave a little. He told us that 250 were present. At the morning service, everyone had been encouraged to double their contribution for the next Sunday. We had a long prayer of thanks to God that night!

November 22, 1963

On November 22, 1963, Dwayne and Jane Davenport barged into the living room quite distraught. "President John F. Kennedy has been assassinated in Dallas, Texas!" Dwayne reported with a very sad voice. He then continued, "Texas Governor John B. Connelly is seriously wounded, and Vice President Lyndon B. Johnson was sworn in as the 36th President of the United States." Jane sat on the couch sobbing. Harold and I were in such total shock that we both felt numb.

"Maybe we can get more information on the Voice of America radio broadcast today or at least tomorrow." Harold replied.

I didn't say anything. I was still stunned.

The Davenports stayed on for an hour or more and we talked extensively about how something like this could happen. We discussed the Martin Luther King, Jr. "I have a dream" speech given last August 28 on the steps at the Lincoln Memorial in Washington, D.C. and we wondered what was going on in America. We had both been so focused on the Ghana Mission effort that all of the other events going on around us seemed blurred. We then joined hands and prayed. Afterwards, the Davenports left.

That night when everyone else was asleep, I sat on the couch to think about the events of the day and to write in my journal. None of this made sense to me. I was bewildered, confused, terrified and uncertain now of our future. This news was so difficult to reconcile. We have been so cut off. Here we were in Africa and the good ole USA was having a black-white conflict. I felt that the whole world was crumbling. I could feel myself getting very angry. This was starting to make sense now why we've had such a difficult time raising funds. My thoughts immediately turned to our recent experiences trying to raise funds for our Ghana missionary work. It was so disappointing. People seemed so uneasy, skeptical, and unwilling to make any commitments. We detected an angry tone in many and couldn't figure out why.

Then I remembered the news coverage of the Martin Luther King Junior "I Have a Dream" speech. I got cold chills wondering if America was on the brink of some gigantic major change, and now I was beginning to wonder if we were in the middle of it. It had suddenly dawned on me how totally unaware and clueless we had been because we were so focused on raising funds and preparing to go to Ghana that we had blocked everything else out of our minds. It was amazing to me what was going on because I could easily remember so many Negro heroes that had blessed my life.

My first remembrance of any interaction with Negros was during the 1940's in my hometown, Terre Haute, Indiana. As a child, my mother invited a wonderful woman, Ivory Spyres, to give my brother and me music lessons. I took piano lessons and my brother took trumpet and drums. We all looked forward to her visit. She was full of life, joyful and after our lessons; she gave us a piano concert. She could make the piano dance—blues, jazz, or any other type of music that we requested. We loved Ivory.

I was able to go all the way through school with the same classmates until the last year of high school when I had gone to summer school every year and graduated six months earlier than the others. So most of the time, I sat next to Cornelius Crawford, a Negro, because we sat in alphabetical order and my name was Critchlow. So I sat behind him. We talked freely every day and discussed the daily lessons.

Then I remembered Ernie Sprinkles. It was 1949 at Wiley High School in Terre Haute, Indiana, during the most important football game of the year. This outstanding, dynamic Negro classmate, with a great talent and love for sports made the deciding touchdown. He had been badly injured in the last quarter of the game, and with the score tied we all cheered wildly as he ran with a broken leg down the field and won the game. He was the school hero!

Harold and I were married in December 1950. We moved to Biloxi, Mississippi. Harold was in the Air Force, and was stationed at Kessler Air Force Base. I was barely eighteen and very naïve. One day in the spring of 1951, I was about three month's pregnant, experiencing morning sickness and was very unsure of my surroundings. We did not have a car. We lived in a little two-room house apartment. We needed groceries and Harold was at work so I decided to go on the bus to the Base Commissary. After I got a couple large sacks of groceries at the Commissary and headed home, I sat at the bus stop terminal to wait on the next bus. When the bus arrived, I just hopped on with my two sacks. After I got home and reached for the house key, I realized that I had left my purse on the seat at the bus stop. I panicked because we had just received our monthly allotment check and all the month's cash was in my purse. I rushed to hail a taxi and headed back to the Base. I prayed!

When I arrived back at the bus terminal, to my great surprise, a Negro Airman was sitting on the bench holding my purse. He looked up at me with gentle unblinking eyes and handed me the large purse. His voice was slow and deliberate, "I waited here for you because I knew how important your purse was."

"Oh, thank you! Thank you!" I replied as I wiped away a tear. *Thank you God!*

The Airman smiled. I quickly paid the taxi driver. The bus stopped. I stepped up onto the bus. The door closed and I watched through the small window on the bus as this Airman disappeared into the distant horizon.

People come into our lives like shooting stars—here for a moment—then gone. God sends them for a purpose, and then they leave. They are bright lights and then they fade away. God knows our future better than we know our past, so God blesses us with these shooting stars. However, we can only see them if we take the time to silently reflect, with thankful hearts, and eyes focused on God.

As my mind sifted through other events in Biloxi, I remembered my very first bus trip. I was alone. I hopped on the empty bus and sat in the very back as this was always my preference. At the next bus stop, a young Negro Airman got on the bus. He stood up for several blocks. There were plenty of seats on the bus, so I motioned for him to sit by me.

I was very shocked when he said to me in a matter-of-fact, slightly angry tone of voice, "Lady, would you please sit in the front of the bus so I can sit down?"

"Why?" I asked looking quite puzzled.

No answer. He just shrugged his shoulders and looked down.

I got up and moved to the front of the bus. He silently took a seat in the back of the bus.

I never did understand why because the entire time I was in school in Indiana, the Negros and the white students always interacted — sat next to each other and talked.

Another experience that made a tremendous impact on me happened in Wiggins, Mississippi, in 1951. Harold was a new Christian and had been asked to preach at the small church in Wiggins. At the end of the service, Harold asked an elderly Negro Christian man in the audience to word the closing prayer. The man led a very powerful, inspiring prayer. After the service was over, the men of the church pounced on Harold angrily demanding that he could not ask a Negro to pray. Then they strongly rebuked Harold. We never went back.

Continuing to reminisce, I turned back the pages of my journal to July 15, 1963, and started reading it. It was a scene in San Diego.

"The mail came early bringing a letter from my brother Jack and his wife. Mother and I both read it at the same time and we both cried. Before I knew it, Mother had bought me a plane ticket to Oakland, California so I could visit with Jack. I was off on a United Jet Mainliner by 2P.M. It happened too fast for me to be scared although this was my very first airplane ride.

I changed planes in Los Angeles and had an hour layover. To pass the time I picked up an old newspaper in the airport waiting area. I eagerly read a story about a civil rights protest in Birmingham, Alabama, in May and a Negro man murdered in June. The next article was about Buddhists riots in South Vietnam after they are denied their celebration of Buddha's birthday. General unrest and the Vietnam situation were much worse.

I was especially interested in the next article about the Congo, 'In February 1961 the Prime Minister Lumumba was assassinated and the country was split into four fragments. In separate incidents, rebels in the Congo killed missionaries Paul Carlson and Irene Ferrell as well as brutalizing missionary doctor Helen Roeselare.'(Lumumba 6/22/2006)

I was unable to finish the article because the flight attendant announced that it was time to board the plane. After I got on the plane, I was still thinking about the articles and wondered how we could manage in Africa.

The only seat on the plane was by a well dressed Negro lady. She warmly smiled and welcomed me to sit with her. She told me her name was Margie Hebert and she said that she was going to Oakland and that her husband would be meeting her at the airport. She smiled and asked me why I was going to Oakland. I told her that I was going to visit my brother whom I hadn't seen in 6 or 7 years and to tell him goodbye before we left for Ghana, West Africa.

Margie then insisted that she wanted to take me to my brother's house from the airport. She said it would be no trouble at all and she insisted. So Margie Hebert and her husband took me in their new Cadillac. It was a very long drive. *I thanked them and also thanked God for the opportunity to meet such a kind couple.* I told my brother, Jack, and he said the cab fare would have cost at least twenty dollars."

As I began to think about my life now in Ghana, I started remembering all the times that God had protected us in the past. I took a deep breath and a comforting feeling blanketed my soul and now I knew that somehow God would solve our present dilemma. I decided to go to bed and let God handle this.

November 28, 1963

Dear Grandma and Grandpa,

My school is fun and exciting. I enjoy my sewing class. I am making Christmas gifts. Thank you so much for the Christmas boxes you are sending us.

Sunday November 24 was a very special day. The Ghana Bible College had a graduation day. It was going to be one hour long, but it turned out to be five hours long.

During church I got very sick. I went to lie down in the car but it was hotter in there. When we got home I was still sick. The next morning I was still sick so I stayed home from school.

After school, Diana went to her girlfriend's birthday party. She said she had a good time. Tuesday I felt better and went to school. People at school come from all over the world, and it is fun to visit in their homes.

Write soon.

Love,
Janice

November 30, 1963

Dear Mother and Daddy,

Last Sunday we drove into the bush to visit the brethren at Kwaso. The church building is a small mud hut, nine by twelve with openings but no screens. We had many flies and mosquitoes. The seats are long wooden benches with no backs. This congregation is unique because all the members are children. The fifteen adult members all fell away but the children remained. Eight children from twelve to fifteen years old are members. However, about sixty children attend regularly. One of the preaching students goes to Kwaso every Sunday to encourage them. Pray for them.

Our children enjoy going to the bush churches. Debbie taught Bible classes in our recent VBS with an interpreter and she really enjoys it. We have almost adjusted to taking the Lord's Supper in glasses that are not too clean and drinking the wine that was poured back into the wine bottle from wine used the previous Sunday.

Recently at one of our most remote bush churches I was so impressed that the preacher took the wine glasses outside to wash them. I later learned the dish water actually came from a urinal and he dried the glasses with a handkerchief stuffed in his back pocket. If we do the best we can to stay healthy, we believe that God will protect us from the germs and keep us well enough to accomplish our mission. Pray for us.

Time is rapidly drawing near for Dwayne and Jane to return to the States and so far no one has agreed to come.

We were saddened to learn about the assassination of President Kennedy. We heard some of the news on the radio on Voice of America.

I feel so relieved tonight. I just got our monthly report in the envelope, stamped and sealed. No more until next month! The bookkeeping here is so complex. I still have about twenty letters to answer and much other typing. We have so many interruptions. John still isn't in school.

Hope you had a wonderful Thanksgiving. Write soon!

Love,
Jane Ann

December 2, 1963

Dear Mother and Daddy,

We received your letter yesterday and were thrilled to hear from you. It is difficult to believe that Christmas is so near. Thank you for sending all the packages. The children will love the toy boxer and the other toys.

Harold and John are going with Dwayne tomorrow to Korforidua in Eastern Ghana. It is about 3 ½ hours drive each way. They will get up early and leave at 5 A.M. They will be home very late. One of the graduate preachers moved there as a missionary to the Aquapim people and they are going to check on his progress. The preacher is 57 years old, is married and has six children. He has been separated from his family for two years in order to attend the Ghana Preacher's School.

Harold has taken many more slides of the Ghana people and the work here. Daddy, would you be able to contact churches in California and to tell about the Ghana work if Harold prepared a color slide report for you to use? You could go in and report on the work and then explain that we need financial help to purchase the microbus plus our return passage to the States. Let us know. The Ghanaians are so receptive to the Gospel but the laborers are few and finances are so scarce. We'll pray for you.

The drums are really talking tonight. We can hear them nearly every night from a nearby village. Write soon!

Love,
Jane Ann

December 13, 1963

Dear Parents,

Thank you for your letters. Today has been quite a day! We hit the jackpot at the Post Office. A Bible Class at Cedars sent us a tape. Terre Haute brethren sent the Terre Haute Tribune paper, children's magazines and news that other boxes were on the way. We never dreamed we would be receiving so many wonderful remembrances. The children are so excited!

We have our Christmas tree up now. The Reynolds left it. The tree is artificial and about 3 feet tall. We brought enough balls from the States to decorate it. We are all enjoying it. The girls are making presents at school for everyone. They sew every Friday, take their lunch and stay until 2, and make many lovely items.

When we came home from shopping, Comfort was in the back yard hanging up clothes. We heard her screaming and we saw John Law running to help her. As she bent over to pick up a clothespin, she saw a snake about 3 feet from her foot. John Law killed the snake with a stick. He said it was a poisonous snake measuring about 24 inches long. Last week John said he saw a snake in the open sewer but we didn't believe him. Glad it didn't bite anyone!

Our garden is doing well. We are enjoying corn on the cob, okra and green beans. We have enjoyed lots of bananas and plantain from off our trees. The ship from America came and now the stores are stocked with many items we have needed for so long.

We are so thrilled. The microbus we ordered in September finally arrived. We drove it home from Accra December 11 on Debbie's birthday. It certainly was the answer to prayers because only four Volkswagens were imported to Ghana. However, two were seriously damaged. We got a perfect one. We thank you, God.

Keep up the prayers. God is answering. Write soon!

Love,
Jane Ann

December 19, 1963

Dear Parents,

We received the letter about Ginger. We checked the Pan Am schedule and she will arrive in Accra tomorrow about noon. We are all going to meet her. We must leave Kumasi about 5 A.M. because it is a good five hours drive to Accra. The children are all excited about the trip. This will be their first trip to "the big city" as a family since we came to Ghana. All the children talk about is bringing Ginger home.

We still haven't received any of the packages you sent. Yesterday we did learn that a boat just came in from America.

Dwayne and Jane are having a Christmas party for all the preachers and their families and for us on December 23. They had us over for a meal last week and served a beautiful birthday cake for Debbie. We had them over to celebrate John's birthday December 7 and Jane's birthday was December 17. One of the Baptist missionary families gave Jane a lovely surprise birthday party. We bought Jane a beautiful cloth for a Ghanaian dress. I bought Diana and me cloth to make us Ghanaian dresses to wear to church services when we go out in the bush.

Daddy, we are so thrilled that you got a hearing aid. Thank you for wanting to present the Ghana slides to congregations around Southern California. We will be praying for you.

Love,
Jane Ann

December 26, 1963

Dear Mother and Daddy,

Hope you had a great Christmas. We had a wonderful sweet Christmas with the best Christmas gift any parent could ask for.

Recently, I bought the children some books with scripts for performing plays. The children studied the books, made costumes out of drapes, sheets, pillowcases and blankets, and all performed a play about the birth of Jesus Christ. I hope you enjoy the picture.

Bye for now. I'll write more soon.

Love,
Jane Ann

Our Best Ever Christmas Gift

Cathy, Janice and John are in their Christmas play costumes. The children presented us a Christmas play telling the story of the birth of Jesus Christ. They made their own costumes and practiced for weeks. Debbie was the reader. Diana was the angel. Janice was Mary and Baby Jesus was a doll. Cathy was a shepherd and John was a wise man.

This is not what I expected!

"He who dwells in the secret place of the Most High shall abide under the shadow of the Almighty. I will say of the Lord, "He is my refuge and my fortress; My God, in Him I will trust."
(Psalms 91: 1-2)

January 1, 1964

Dear Mother and Daddy,

Happy New Year! We had the Davenports over last night. Harold made the best pecan rolls and Swedish fruit bread and we had goodies out of a box sent from the brethren in Terre Haute. After the children went to bed at ten o'clock, the Davenports and the Derrs had a real exciting game of Canasta.

So happy you got a new projector to show the Ghana slides. Harold is busy putting together a series of slides showing the interesting customs and daily life of the Ghanaian people. We have some beautiful slides of the cocoa industry. The series will also have maps.

I had to postpone finishing this letter. I had to get the Ghana Report and Financial Statements ready to mail to Wilmington.

Ginger did not come in as expected. After much research and a cablegram to the Derrs, we located Ginger in Accra. She is really a world traveler. The airlines put her in a kennel in New York for 10 days and then flew her BOAC to London. After a few days, she was flown to Accra. We arranged for her to fly to Kumasi today.

We thank you for helping to bring Ginger here and thank you for helping to raise funds for our trip home. Write soon.

Love,
Jane Ann

John was so happy to have our Boxer pup, Ginger with us again.
We found the other puppy, Nutmeg in Ghana.

January 6, 1964

Dear Grandma and Grandpa Critchlow,

Ginger is with us again. She is very happy here. She likes to chase lizards very much. The lizards climb up the wall of the vacant house next door and Ginger gets very mad.

We are out two weeks for a school vacation. We went to Accra to get Ginger. When we got to Accra, we were surprised to find out that Ginger was not there. Last Saturday Daddy flew back to Accra to get her. Ginger had gotten very big since we last saw her. She got to fly in the cockpit with the pilot because she was too big to fit in a dog carrier. Daddy talked a long time to get the pilot to take Ginger.

We are having another VBS. Debbie and Mommy are teaching the pre-school children. I am not helping because I am in school. John is very anxious to go to school. God willing he will be able to go soon.

Mommy's birthday is the 14th. I am going to get her a present. Debbie is making Mommy a crocheted present.

I'll write more soon.

Love,
Janice

January 9, 1964

Dear Mother and Daddy,

We just received your letter today dated December 30. We still have not received the boxes yet but we do have Ginger. She was on the road three weeks instead of the 72 hours we were promised. She went to Chicago by train and flew the next day to New York. They kept her in a kennel for ten days; then flew her to London for a few days. She then flew to Accra and was there several days. Harold finally flew to Accra last Saturday to get her. They did not send her because they lost the papers we sent them three weeks ago. Her crate was too large to get into a Ghana Airways plane so Harold convinced the pilot to let her ride without a crate. She ended up riding in front in the pilot's cabin. The pilot was British.

The Ghanaians are really afraid of Ginger. Most of the dogs here are very small. Ginger lost some weight but appears to be in good health. She is enjoying the excitement here. She killed a chicken her first day here. She loves to chase the lizards and now we have no lizard problem. We take her with us Sundays out in the bush and she loves it. Whenever we get into the car, she thinks she must go too. The children spend much time playing with her. Harold loves her the most. Ginger is quite partial to Harold. She just shakes all over as she wags her tail every time Harold calls her. We thank you so much for bringing her over here.

We are in the midst of a VBS at Old Tafo. We had 166-167 the last two days. I am teaching a class of pre-school children. Debbie helped the first three days. She's in school now. The children at VBS do not speak any English. Emmanuel interpreted for me and taught them Twi songs. We have about 56 each day. They listen quietly and are very good. Our class is outside under a brush arbor. The children are not all under five. Some are older but have never attended school. We had three mothers. I used the flannel board that you gave us. The children love it. Debbie is getting to be a great teacher. I'm really proud of her.

Harold has been gone every night this week. Two religious groups approached our preachers wanting to know more about New Testament Christianity. They are not happy with the way they have been worshipping. We anticipate baptizing many adults from both groups. The road is only barely wide enough for one car and grass is growing up in the middle of the road. About 150 to 200 adults have been attending. In such a preaching service, you have two interpreters. One interpreter is for the sermon and the other reads all the Scriptures in Twi. Pray that one or two men from this group will be able to attend the Bible Training School.

Did I tell you that Emmanuel's wife had a baby girl recently and they named her Jane Ann? This is their sixth child. Write soon.

Love,
Jane Ann

January 17, 1964

Dear Mother and Daddy,

We enjoyed your last letter. Ginger is still enjoying chasing the lizards. They seem to be disappearing fast while Ginger gains weight.

I had a great birthday. Harold and the girls baked me a pretty birthday cake and filled the top with 31 candles. I can't believe I am that old! Time flies.

It looks very favorable about the two groups of people wanting to know more about New Testament Christianity. Their preachers are enrolling in our Bible Correspondence Courses! Five of the group who previously took the Bible Courses were baptized.

We have two letters on our desk now from people wanting to be baptized—this is wonderful, however it lays a heavy burden on our hearts as both live great distances from Kumasi in opposite directions. Who is able to go? Who is able to encourage and strengthen them after they are baptized? The work in Kumasi is undermanned now and we cannot accept all the doors of opportunity here—no workers and little money. Pray for them. Over 10,000 people have completed at least one of the four Bible Courses we offer. Many respond wanting to be baptized and no one to follow-up. Quite a challenge! The Baptists have more missionaries in Lagos, Nigeria than the church of Christ has in the whole world. So many preachers in America are preaching to people who don't want to hear the gospel.

Daddy, thanks for showing the Ghana films.

Love,
Jane Ann

Albert Larbi works diligently everyday grading Bible Correspondence Lessons. We had about 10,000 students from Ghana and many other African nations.

This small building behind our house is used as the Bible Correspondence Office, a small dispensary/storage room and a classroom.

January 22, 1964

Dear Grandma and Grandpa,

We got the very nice tape today. We really enjoy the music. As you know, Tennessee Ernie Ford is our favorite singer.

Guess what? I can make pies now. Diana doesn't like it either because she learned to make them before I did. Daddy told me that my pies were the best, but of course, not in front of her.

I was thinking about the word FORD and guess what I learned today. F—fix O—or R—repair D—daily. We got a box from Grandma and Grandpa Derr and I got the most clothes of anyone. I think it is because when I grow out of it, it will go down the line, and that way it goes farther.

Daddy has gone boat crazy lately. He has started making another model boat. He said that he may make me one for my birthday. At least it's not a dump truck. We went to the movies last night and we saw Robin Hood and the pirates. Diana, Janice and Cathy didn't go because they went to a slumber party. I think that was why we went because that way it's half the normal price and we can get soda pop and candy too.

Thanks again for the nice tape with music on it. Tell everyone "Hi" and Denny Fincher too.

Lots of Love,
Debbie

January 30, 1964

Dear Mother and Daddy,

Just a brief update on the political situation here since you asked. We read this in the New York Times.

"On January 24, Ghana became a member of the Communist family of nations by a so-called election which was a mockery of anything called democratic. People were forced to vote when police came into their homes and compelled them to vote yes for a one-party socialist state.

Many of the polling stations contained one ballot box which was marked "yes". In polling stations with two ballot boxes the "no" box was placed in a separate room with police guards. By unanimous vote, Ghana became a socialist state.

Many fruits of communism are already beginning to bear fruit: the enforcement of forced labor which the ruling party calls communal labor. Many people are heavily fined or imprisoned because they refuse to take part in communal labor projects that include building roads, government buildings, and party headquarters in the various districts.

All Ghana's borders remain closed. Suspicion reigns between Ghana and her neighbors: Ivory Coast, Togo and Upper Volta. It is reported that 2,000 to 3,000 persons are imprisoned under the Preventative Detention Act.

In December 1963, President Nkrumah dismissed Chief Justice Sir Arku Korsah when the judge acquitted five high Government officials who had been charged with treason. These officials are now on trial behind closed doors.

As the economy falters, government controls tighten, and so life is becoming increasingly difficult here.

The bitterest anti-American campaign so far is continuing and the United States is now called, "Fascist-imperialist", New York Times reports that Western diplomats here say Ghanaians, who were once forthright and friendly are now subdued and distant and that officials rarely accept social invitations. Some are taking the position that anyone who associates with Americans is an enemy of socialism."(New York Times 1/24/1964)

We hope that we are able to stay because the work here is progressing so well. Recently 21 obeyed the gospel and accepted Jesus Christ as their Savior. One man traveled 165 miles just to be baptized.

Thanks for your prayers and help in raising our return travel funds. Will write more soon.

Love,
Jane Ann

February 1, 1964

Dear Mother and Daddy,

This is Saturday morning. The children are all out in the garage in the "classroom" playing school and singing songs. The girls have a girlfriend over to visit. She is Canadian and her father is a Mennonite missionary. They plan to leave Ghana for good in June. This is their second tour.

Harold is still working on the pictures for you to show to churches. It takes so long since we must send them to England to get them developed.

Harold took John with him one evening preaching to Odumanago. The access road is only passable during certain times of the year, and at its best is only wide enough for one car. Immediately after they arrived, they were swamped with children and adults who could not take their eyes off of John. A.K., the Ghanaian preacher with them, explained that these people had never seen a white child before. Although John is not in a formal school, he is really getting an education! He is Harold's little apprentice in every job Harold undertakes. He loves to go out in the bush evenings with Harold and the preachers to preach. The girls and I usually stay home.

In January classes were resumed at the Bible Training School. Our house is a very busy place now! We always have people coming and going all of the time. Harold has a lot of counseling sessions with preachers in our living room between 7A.M. and 8A.M. We have tried hard to keep a schedule but we get so frustrated that it seems best to take each day and its many challenges in stride and make the best of it. The rule of the day is interruptions. It is critical that we do not rush the people and always exhibit kindness as they are always potential preachers and new Christians.

Everything here is a problem. Our washing machine is broken. Harold tried to get a repair man to fix it but he said he cannot get the part we need. It will need to be ordered from Europe. Then he said something about waiting for import license to be renewed to be able to order the part. If we should decide to buy another washer—there are none for sale now in Kumasi. It appears that we need to adjust to waiting three months to purchase an article. God is trying to teach us patience. Our boxes are still not here that you sent and none of the other missionaries have their Christmas boxes yet.

When Harold mailed the slides to you, I thought Harold was going to explode with anger. He waited at the Post Office about an hour in three different lines. When he was sent to the fourth line which was at least a block long—he came home and went back the next day to mail it.

I got the monthly reports out last night and feel greatly relieved. I never thought that I would be doing bookkeeping here without an adding machine or a calculator and with no training—and then trying to convert shillings and pence into American currency. Sure wish I had taken bookkeeping or accounting in school.

Our garden is doing well and we are enjoying lots of green beans, lettuce, cucumbers and radishes. Write soon!

Love,
Jane Ann

February 5, 1964

Dear Mother and Daddy,

We enjoyed your letter. This is Friday evening and I thought I would write while everything is quiet.

Harold just left to take a car load of preachers to Koforidua, which is a 3 ½ hour drive each way. They plan a big preaching effort in response to the Bible Correspondence Course results. Many have completed the courses and want to learn more. I will feel a lot better when Harold gets home because it is a very bad road and especially at night. Harold was exhausted before he left because of the preaching excursion on Wednesday night.

Dwayne and Jane Davenport are on a vacation in Northern Ghana so we are very busy covering for them, plus our own work. Then Comfort didn't come today. She was sick. I finally got the housework done and then made some whole wheat bread. We eat homemade bread now most of the time. We especially enjoy the stone ground wheat.

When we were at the store a couple of weeks ago, the bread truck was unloading that delicious bread in the plastic bags. Originally the bread came unwrapped thrown in a dirty truck bed and the grocery store people put the bread in the plastic bags just before it was sold to keep it fresh. Now we make all of our own bread!

We are still organizing the pictures. We do have a lot of pictures but we do not have the complete story yet that Harold wants to tell. We will send them soon.

We are all well now. Last week I had a bad chest cold. I am really behind in the office work. I must type up a lot of stencils for the mimeograph machine. Since the Ghana Bible College has started again, Harold is making seven work books for the students. I am typing the Old Testament Survey, the New Testament history, and geography. It is a lot of work but the preachers will get so much good out of the workbooks and retain a lot more. They meet three mornings a week in our garage. Harold fixed this up for a classroom. The students come early to study and have access to Harold's books in his office.

The work is going along very well. We plan to go out into the bush Sunday. One of the preachers has arranged for us to attend a fetish meeting at the fetish temple. That same day a big festival is planned in Kumasi with 100 chiefs attending and they will show the public the historic Golden Stool. The Ashanti nation has a very historical and colorful story and we are right in the middle of it. They were the last tribe in West Africa to be conquered by the British and this was not until 1940. We purchased the best book yesterday, "The Religion and Art of the Ashanti People". It is very interesting to read. I must close. Write soon.

Love,
Jane Ann

February 11, 1964

Greetings from Ghanaland!

We are all well and the work is going along great. Sunday was a very busy and eventful day. First, we visited one of the most remote congregations in the bush. When Harold and John went there recently, the people all stared at John. After Harold was finished preaching, the Ghanaians said that John was the first white child they had ever seen. They paid a lot of attention to us Sunday. I wore my Ghanaian dress. This always gets a warm reception from all the women.

One of the women who attended services announced that she praised the Lord because we had come to preach Jesus Christ to her town. She is not a Christian yet but she knows that God sent us there. She has two houses and is letting the church use one of her houses for services. She asked for prayers and said that all of her families were idol worshippers. Then she again praised God that we had come. This is a new congregation of four members and is one month old.

We then rushed to Kumasi to attend the Adaekesie festival which is only held every four years. Otumfuo the Asantehene, Sir Osei Agyeman Prempeh II is the big chief of the Ashanti Tribe which was the former Ashanti Nation. He was the main attraction, and sat in state for more than five hours to receive all the fifty chiefs of the Kumasi

Traditional Area as well as distinguished guests who attended the ceremony. The ceremony was marked by traditional drumming and dancing. Thousands attended. Otumfuo, the Asantehene rode in a richly decorated palanquin from his palace to the durbar or festival. It was a very colorful and rare experience. We were privileged to get many pictures.

A Ghanaian Chief and his Regalia

A Ghanaian chief considers it extremely important to observe all the traditional festivals. The stools and swords are believed to be inhabited by the souls of the ancestors. At the festivals a cleansing ritual takes place. This is believed to cleanse the stools, swords and the entire chiefdom. The ancestors are fed with the first fruits of the fields or from the first catch, and prayers are offered to them or through them to the Supreme Deity.

When the worship of the ancestors is finished, the chief, their living representative, sits in state with all the pomp and pageantry his regalia provides, to receive the homage of his people and in return to extend to them hospitality and bestow gifts. Drumming, dancing, merriment and feasting abounds.

The stool, sword or linguist-stick, or whatever it may be—helps, as a symbol, to give reality or intelligibility to what a people believe to be the explanation of life upon earth and life after death. It is this explanation of the whole life—meaning life not interrupted.

Umbrella

State umbrellas are used by chiefs in all parts of Ghana as cano-pies and as another symbol of their office. The idea of a canopy naturally originated from the ordinary use of an umbrella as protec-tion against rain and sun. The large ceremonial umbrellas are manu-factured locally from different kinds of beautifully colored textiles: silk, felt, brocade, damask and kente. On the top of the umbrella is usually placed a carved symbol of some saying or message, wrapped in silver or gold leaf like the shape of a state sword. The Asantehene has no fewer than twenty-three different umbrellas.

Palanquins

An English soldier, who saw a palanquin for the first time, called it a stretcher on which Ghana chief's rode. It is a kind of litter or hammock in which chiefs of Southern Ghana are carried when they appear in state. Chiefs, who are privileged to do so, decorate the outside of their palanquins with felt cloth and leopard skin. It is usual for a chief seated in a palanquin to be followed by drummers. The chief then dances on the palanquin to the rhythm of the music. Sometimes he dances with a gun and a sword in his hands. The carriers of the state umbrellas make them flutter to the rhythm of the music. (Kyerematen 89-92)

The preachers in the Ghana Bible College are studying the Old Testament Survey that Harold put together. They are learning many valuable lessons and are beginning to apply these to their culture.

One preacher, E.A. Asante was extremely interested in the story about Moses and Aaron pleading with the Egyptian Pharaoh to release the Israelites and let them go home.

Asante asked, "God gave Moses and Aaron power to do wondrous things. However, the Pharaoh's priests had power also. Do you believe that Satan gives his power to those individuals he chooses?"

"Asante, 1 John 4 tells us to test the spirits to see which ones are from God," Harold replied.

Asante then invited us to go with him to his mother's village to celebrate a dubar festival honoring the god of fertility. At daybreak on Saturday morning, our entire family packed into the VW microbus with Asante. Harold drove and Asante guided us down a narrow dirt road through dense bush to a small village. We saw a large, beautiful two-story white concrete block house as we approached the village. The house was surrounded by a large white fence with a fancy gate; a new black Buick Roadmaster car was parked in front of the house.

Asante gave us a brief sketch of the background of the fetish priest and his assistants. The fetish priest was a graduate of Oxford University and his assistants were all college graduates. Asante emphasized that this priest is a very wealthy man and in fact owned this town.

When we arrived at the house gate, three young priests warmly greeted us and took us inside the house. We were treated with much kindness and served an orange soft drink. All the other guests in the house were served zombies, which is an alcoholic drink with Schnapps and canned milk. The radio was playing loud jazzy music. After visiting with us a few minutes, the fetish priest excused himself to prepare for the festival.

Soon the priest came out with gold toga, gold bracelets, rings over his arms and hands, and a golden wreath on his head. He shook everyone's hand and asked us to remain in the house while he marched through the town under a giant umbrella with his three helpers.

We went outside and watched as the group marched about three or four blocks to the festival grounds. Other men marched along side of them firing shot guns in the air. We then followed them to the grounds with the other guests and were shown choice seats under a U-shaped brush arbor. In the middle was a large platform and behind it was a round concrete house with a thatched roof. All the priests went inside of the house. The fetish priest's six wives entered the arbor. They all sat together on wooden benches in the front row. All were dressed alike in elaborate gold Ghanaian dresses. Two of the priest's small children were dressed for the occasion as they played their roles in the elaborate drama. Behind the house several men fired many shots.

The fetish priest came out of the house after an hour dressed in new attire. This was supposed to represent the fetish god Kwakye. His costume consisted of a pink fancy hooped knee-length skirt and a white lace ruffled top. A pointed black and gold hat was perched on top of his head. He acted drunk after all of those zombies. The three assistants helped him onto the platform to a rocking chair covered with a velvet carpet. He rocked and his assistants mopped his brow. Afterward they gave him a drink in a little green glass.

We took pictures and bid the younger priest goodbye. However, they informed us that we must stay. They announced over the loud speaker system, "The foreign guests are requested to stay so that we may entertain you to the fullest."

We stayed. They were kind to pose for pictures. Next the young priests carried the fetish priest in his rocking chair on the platform through the town to another larger place where more celebrations took place. We were again ushered to choice seats and served a cool orange soft drink. The others were served zombies. We were asked to walk by and to greet the fetish priest. Next we took our seats and watched the drummers, dancers, and the band. Afterward the fetish priest was carried to a platform and he poured out libations. Libations is pouring an alcoholic beverage on the ground or sacrificing something to appease the ancestral spirits and evil spirits. A few years ago human sacrifices were made.

The fetish priest was then carried by the younger priests to his sanctuary so that he could change into another costume which represented the god James. We asked permission to leave again and were denied. In ten minutes we asked permission again to leave. They were very kind and let us take more pictures and explained what all the pictures meant. We then left.

Only the Gospel of Jesus Christ has the power to free men from the burden of that kind of religion. We have quite a challenge in Ghana.

Love,
Jane Ann

P.S. A lot of people are praying fervently for us!

We received the most thrilling news today. A church in Tulsa, Oklahoma, had a special prayer service for us! Diana and Janice have been corresponding with a children's Bible Class there. The class sent $6 for the bus. Afterwards the elders decided to start sending us $15 each month regular support. We have never met them. A Bible class in Costa Mesa, California, wrote telling us that they are praying for us. They are going to send monthly support from the children's Bible Class.

A Fetish Priest at the Fetish Festival

This is a picture of a fetish priest sitting under the decorated platform. Several of his priests are carrying him through the town.

Some of his assistants are shaking shakers and behind him several men are beating drums. The fetish religion teaches that evil spirits are in the trees, water, and ground trying to do harm to the people. The fetish priest appeases these spirits by pouring libations. Libations consist of pouring an alcoholic drink, mixed with blood, on the ground. At this time, it is chicken blood, however, in earlier days, human sacrifice was practiced. Fetish beliefs also include ancestral worship.(Kyerematen 101-112)

This is a picture of a thrashed roof structure in the background and a large platform in the front to the right of the picture. The fetish priest sat on the top of the large platform and performed some of his rituals.

March 4, 1964

Dear Mother and Daddy,

We were glad to get your letters. I have been slow in writing because I've had so much office work to do. I just got the monthly report in the mail. I'm still typing stencils for Bible lessons for the Ghana Bible College, and writing to people hoping to get more monthly support. I dream of some new invention to produce these reports as it is so tedious typing on the stencils. They are blue waxed material and it is so difficult to correct mistakes. The old duplicator is so slow copying the pages and sometimes the ink smudges.

You should be receiving the slides about April 15. The last slides should arrive here from England about March 16. It will take Harold about a week to record the narration on the tape. Afterwards I will type out the explanation. We will mail the packet to Cedars in Wilmington and have them make duplicate copies and mail you a set. Cedars will try raising funds on the east coast. You can try to raise funds on the west coast. The Cedars Church is also sending a set to George Forsythe in Terre Haute, Indiana. He has agreed to try to raise funds in the Midwest. We are praying for success.

Harold just came in and said he is sure going to need your help in raising funds. The Davenports are returning to the States June 1 and no one will be replacing them. So we will need at least an additional $300 per month now to cover Davenports work here.

Our ship finally came in yesterday. We received two boxes from you. Both of these boxes were in excellent condition. The boxes contained: boy's sweater, girl's sweaters, skirts, boy's pants, 1 stapler and staples, umbrella set, 2 pair cotton pajamas, gown, 3 diaries and drapes. Thank you so much. We are all well now.

Love,
Jane Ann

March 9, 1964

Dear Mother and Daddy,

It hardly seems possible that we have been here six months. We feel the hardest part is over—that drastic adjustment to the cultural shock. Time passes by swiftly because we are so deeply involved in the work.

A great opportunity has been presented to us. Our landlord is building a house next door to the house where we live. The two houses are very close together. He offered to rent the new house to the church for a reasonable amount. He promised to build a big servants quarters in the back and put a wall around both houses.

The house where we live would make a perfect church building. The living-dining room is 16 feet by 36 feet. This could be an auditorium to seat 150-200 people. This could also be used for classes for the Ghana Bible College. The four bedrooms and the kitchen could be used for dormitories to sleep 12 students. The servant's quarters could house students and the garage that is now being used for the Bible College could be used as a Bible classroom and also a place to teach illiterate adults to read. One of the student preachers is a school teacher. He wants to start this project. He wants to use Bible material as text books for the students to practice their reading skills.

It is so important to have a Bible Training School here. At the present time in Kumasi, a city of 221,000 people, the Church of Christ has only two congregations. One congregation is meeting in a building consisting of six posts holding up a corrugated tin roof on a concrete slab. The other congregation meets in a brush arbor in front of one of the member's houses.

The house where we live is very close to the Kwame Nkrumah University and a church in this location could do much to reach people living in the University compound since the other two congregations are a great distance from here. This house is in front of the 6 ½ acres the Ghana Government gave to the church for the purpose of constructing a church building, a Bible Training School, and two missionary houses.

It will take great faith to plan this work as our bank account was overdrawn according to our last letter from Cedars. We need your prayers. Comfort said, "The Lord will provide."

Davenports are packing, selling, and getting ready to leave June 1. Still no one has volunteered to come. So it looks like we will be here alone. No really. God will be here with us. We have so many people praying for us.

We have decided not to attend church services in town on Sunday nights. Instead, we will devote this time to our family Bible classes. The reason we made this choice is because we cannot understand anything spoken—everything is in Twi. It is not fair to the children. Last night we had our first study at home. We used workbooks. Harold teaches the older three girls and I teach Cathy and John.

91

The children are very eager to learn. We discovered that the daily morning devotional was just not enough for them. Little John amazes me with his ability to remember facts. He says, "Mommy, I want to learn about God." When Harold goes out to preach in the evenings, usually he takes John with him. However, if John stays home with me, he gets out his book about the life of David Livingstone and insists that I read to him.

Thank you so much for the boxes. It was such an exciting time as everyone helped to open up the boxes and peek inside to discover the wonderful treasures. Write soon.

Love,
Jane Ann

March 6, 1964

Dear Bible Class,

This is Diana Derr. I am 10 years old. We live in Ghana, West Africa. We are missionaries. I have three sisters and one brother. I go to Ridge School. My teacher is British. On Friday afternoons, we have a two hour sewing class after school. We are now learning to knit. I like to knit. I like school very much. One of my girl friends came from Ceylon, and one from Australia, and one from Canada.

It is the dry season now. They say this year is not as hot as usual. The rainy season will start sometime in March and will continue until about October.

About every Sunday we go out in the bush. The bush is like a big field of grass, bushes, and trees with big palm leaves. Last month we went out to what we call bush-bush. When we got there everybody stared at us. This is because the people had never ever seen any white children.

When services were over, we went back to Kumasi and attended the Adaekesie Festival. This festival only comes one time every four years. The Ashantehene is what you might call the king of the Ashantis. He was always in the front of the festival. Daddy got a picture of him. A man invited Daddy into the chief's circle. The chief wore kente and gold. Kente cloth is a beautiful kind of cloth that the people weave by hand. It will take about nine months to weave a chief's cloth. About all the chiefs were carried in litters under umbrellas. The umbrellas were very large and were made of beautiful bright colored velvet and satin. We stayed there a little while, went home, got a bite to eat and hurried to a place in the bush.

We went to a fetish festival. A fetish priest is a man who thinks he is a representative of a god and can make intercession to appease the evil spirits and the spirits of the people's ancestors. He poured some alcoholic drink on the ground to appease the evil spirits. This is called libations. A few years ago they even killed little children to sacrifice to appease the evil spirits. They do not know about Jesus.

When it was about 6:00 P.M. we left. That evening at church, we had filmstips about "The Life of Christ". We like it here very much.

In Christian Love,
Diana Lynn Derr

March 13, 1964

This morning as I was typing in our bedroom-office, suddenly one of those violent tropical storms erupted. The hard rain pounded on the tin roof and sounded like an army of men pounding nails on top of us. The girls were all in school, and John was with Harold running errands. Comfort was in the kitchen working. Little Jerry was tied to her back. The rain woke Jerry up and he started to cry. We both met in the living room to watch the storm.

"Are there many storms here during the rainy season?" I questioned as I watched Comfort gently patting little Jerry as he slowly closed his eyes.

"Most of the big storms come at the beginning and end of the rainy season." Comfort replied as she swayed back and forth rocking Jerry to sleep.

The storm ended as abruptly as it began. Shortly after, we could hear the sounds of many lorries buzzing by on the road in front of our house. I went out on the front porch to watch as the lorries passed by and the passengers swayed back and forth on the long board seats singing and drumming.

Comfort followed me out on the porch and questioned," Why do you always stop your work to watch the lorries as they pass by?"

"I enjoy so much the singing and drumming!" I answered as I started to question myself.

"Why do you think this is strange?" she added as she closely observed my reaction.

When I did not immediately answer her, Comfort continued, "Aren't people in American happy? Why don't they sing?"

I had no answer for Comfort.

Two hours later, John Law rushed to the front door. He pounded the door loudly and shouted excitedly. When I opened the door, I saw John Law shaking and holding Ginger.

"What happened?" I sobbed.

Comfort quickly came out to interpret. John Law was explaining that a passing lorrie ran over Ginger. John Law bent over and laid Ginger's body at my feet on the living room floor. He explained to Comfort that we should keep Ginger inside the house because several men who were passing by inquired if they could buy Ginger's body to use her for food! I was stunned! Comfort and John Law went outside to continue the conversation.

I stood alone in the house watching Ginger as her body jerked and blood poured out. She was dying and I couldn't do anything to stop it.

Crazy thoughts kept racing through my mind. How can I tell the children? Where are Harold and John? Looking at my watch, I realized that I had several hours to collect my thoughts before the girls came home from school. *Why? Ginger? Why?* I could feel the tears starting to roll down my cheeks. Then I started sobbing. *Why?*

A few minutes later, Harold entered the house. Albert Larbi, one of the preachers had stopped Harold as he pulled in the driveway and told him the story. John Law then took John out to help him in the garden. He knew how much John loved Ginger and how devastating this was going to be when he found out.

As Harold gave me a comforting hug and wiped tears from my cheeks, he explained, "Sweetheart, don't cry over spilled milk." He continued "We don't have time to cry now. We can cry later. Get me a towel. I need to hurry and bury Ginger before the girls get home, and John Law brings John back."

Returning with an armload of towels, I questioned, "Harold, how do we tell the children?"

No answer.

When Harold returned from burying Ginger, I could feel his anger, frustration and deep sorrow. "I can't risk telling the children where I buried Ginger," he said with downcast eyes. "They might go there" he added with his direct matter-of-fact voice. "If anyone finds her they will dig her up and eat her." Slowly he walked away as his words faded into the distance, "I'm going to pick up the girls at school. I'll take John and then tell the children on the way home."

I turned around as Comfort came into the room with the mop. As we busied ourselves cleaning the floor before the children got home, I felt a calmness surrounding me as I prayed for reassuring words for the children.

After the evening meal, we all sat silently around the table.

"Daddy," said John slowly, "Do dogs go to heaven?"

Harold looked up quite unprepared to answer as he slowly scratched his head.

"It's not fair!" interrupted Janice, her face red and fists clenched. "We worked so hard to get Ginger here."

"She was part of our family," Diana added as she chewed her lip to keep the tears inside.

Debbie leaned back in her chair. With downcast eyes, she slowly added, "How are we going to tell our grandparents? Grandma Derr even gave Ginger iced tea." She shook her head and continued, "They sacrificed so much to bring Ginger here."

Harold scratched his head again and cleared his throat.

"I want to go home and see Grandma!" Cathy blurted out.

"We can't go home," Diana replied in a matter-of-fact voice, "because we don't have the money!"

"Daddy, is that true?" Janice questioned with her eyes demanding a quick answer.

"Harold, why don't we all pray?" I said as I gestured to Harold to begin the prayer. We all joined hands and prayed.

March 15, 1964

Dear Mother and Daddy,

Yesterday morning, Harold chose for his sermon the familiar story of Abraham offering his son as a sacrifice to God. He emphasized the providential care of God, and the faith that Isaac had in God. Abraham and Isaac did not fight, but trusted the will of God. As Abraham raised his knife to kill his son, God stayed his hand.

Last night one of the preaching students, Harold and John left in the VW to conduct worship services at Gyegyie, about 6 miles west of Kumasi. Just before they reached the Gyegyie turn off an oncoming gasoline truck exploded before their eyes. They were the nearest vehicle to the explosion but were unharmed. The truck exploded four or five times and both men inside the truck burned to death. No other cars were involved. It just exploded. A few seconds more and the VW would have burned up too. Yes, God "stayed Harold's foot" and they are all safe, but brought much closer to the reality of death, and the providential care of God. We are so thankful we have a praying church behind us.

The color slide report is finished and we are mailing it to Cedars today. This report is 35 minutes long. It has 72 pictures and also has an audio tape with it. We also are sending a typed narration so anyone can use what is best for the situation. We will have you a copy made plus one for the Derr's to use in Terre Haute, Indiana. We were very pleased with the result.

I made a Children's Ghana Report for use in Bible Classes for children five to twelve years old. Cathy and John each sang a song. Janice is the speaker. We will mail this today to Cedars. They will be sending you a copy.

I must close for now. Write soon.

Love,
Jane Ann

Late in March 1964

It was one of those nights during the rainy season when I couldn't sleep. Harold was exhausted and went to bed early. He works so hard. I'm so concerned about him. He seems to be sick so much here. Malaria and the heat have really taken a toll on his health and energy level. He enjoys sleeping with the rain pounding on the tin roof. I very carefully got out of bed and tiptoed to the back bedroom window. The house was L-shaped and we could look through our bedroom window and see where Cathy and John slept. The light was on tonight and I could see Cathy reading a bedtime story to John. Tonight she was reading "Mrs. Lees Stories About Jesus".

My heart swelled with thankfulness as I watched. The rain stopped. I went softly back to bed. I thanked God. I continued my prayer by pretending that all of my daily anxieties, problems and concerns were in separate colored balloons. As I visualized each problem balloon floating away one by one, I released them into God's outstretched arms. After all of the balloons floated upward and out of sight, I fell asleep.

April 15, 1964

Dear Mother and Daddy,

I couldn't find time to write before now. Harold was very sick for ten days. We think it was malaria. He got a stronger malaria medication and feels much better now. He had been working night and day and was completely exhausted when the malaria hit. After all at 35, you can't keep the same pace as you did in your twenties. We reorganized some of the work. Now everything is going much smoother.

In March, 18 were baptized and over 600 enrolled in the Bible Correspondence Courses. Already this month nine have been baptized and the Bible Correspondence School continues to expand in many parts of Ghana and to neighboring countries. The big challenge now is not having enough workers and finding money for postage. Debbie, Diana and Janice are grading papers every day and enjoying it very much. It is greatly increasing their Bible knowledge. It is a 12 lesson Bible course on Bible fundamentals. It certainly makes the girls feel that they are a vital part of the work.

We all look forward to our Sunday night Bible class. I teach Cathy and John about the Life of Christ using Journeys through the Bible Workbooks. Cathy knows six or seven memory verses and John knows three. Harold teaches Debbie, Diana and Janice using a workbook on the Church. Then the older girls teach Cathy and John a Bible class once a week using various workbooks here. This makes four hours of Bible study each week. We appreciate our Bible Class teachers much more now. Mother, I didn't realize how hard you have worked teaching Bible to second grade students for 17 years. Quite a challenge, but you always made it look so easy.

Debbie isn't getting along well with her school work at the University School. We are taking her out of school. We have ordered the Calvert Correspondence Course from the States. I am going to teach her at home. She will miss her friends at school, but we will try to make up this void with other interesting activities like sewing, crocheting, knitting, and oil painting. I plan to get her a typing book and teach her typing. Diana turned eleven April 4. So next March will be her last month at the British school. Looks like I'll be going back to school—teaching two at home.

Now you probably have the Ghana slides. I'm attaching a list of churches for you to contact. We haven't heard about anyone replacing the Davenports.

Harold is planning to have a VBS at each of the congregations with a gospel meeting each night. Two preaching students and two preachers will spend six days in each area. They will use the same material at each congregation. They will gather up the books at the end of each class and use them at the next congregation. This will be held this summer when the Bible College is not in session. These preachers usually work in the Bible Correspondence School but Debbie, Diana and Janice will take over this work so the preachers can conduct VBS. Yes, our children are a vital part of the work here.

I'm giving Diana a birthday party today. It will be an afternoon tea from 4 to 6. Diana enjoys wearing her Ghanaian dress to church. She enjoys the work here. Write soon.

Love,
Jane Ann

Diana, Debbie and Janice are grading Bible Correspondence Lessons.

This is a picture of Diana's birthday party guests. In addition to Debbie, Janice, Cathy and John, many of Diana's classmates from Ridge School, a private British School came to the party.

*Jane Ann, Diana and John enjoyed wearing their Ghanaian
garments to church services.*

Sunday April 19, 1964

Dear Mother and Daddy,

I have a thirty minute break before we leave for church. We are
going to the "bush-bush" congregation at Dumanaffo. Harold is over
the malaria now. He had Iron and Vitamin B shots and takes stronger
malaria medicine now.

Sunday Afternoon

I was interrupted, as usual, this morning, so I will try to finish your letter now. We are home from Dumanoffo, have eaten lunch, the girls are cleaning up the kitchen, and Harold is asleep. He still tires out so easily after his sickness.

The morning was very challenging. The church had been meeting in a room that belonged to an idol worshipper. The wife wanted us to meet there. The husband prevented us. We met outside under a tree in the marketplace. Someone got into a fight on the other side of the tree. Another religious group tried to prevent us from conducting our service. They paraded around and around the tree singing and dancing. Afterwards, a man, who is currently studying with the preacher, volunteered the use of his new house for next Sunday.

Thank you so much for showing the Ghana slides. I know that God will bless your efforts because the work cannot go on here without financial assistance. The people are really suffering and the opportunity to teach about Christ was never greater. More people here are attending religious services than ever before as they sing, "Our father's worshipped idols and it profited them nothing. As for me, I will serve God."

Albert Larbi, one of the preaching students and a former school teacher, has started a class at Amakon three nights a week to teach illiterate adults to read and write Twi, the local language. This is a Christian service that is extended free of charge by the church in Amakon due to Albert Larbi's suggestion and efforts. He has trained his fellow preacher, Evans Danquah to conduct a similar class at Semfie. The Semfie Town Council was so thrilled to have this Christian service offered for the people of the town. They are making it mandatory that all illiterate adults in Semfie must attend this class. The first night 45 attended. The books are provided by the United Nations Educational Branch.

We still do not know if anyone will replace the Davenports.

Love,
Jane Ann

This is a typical road that we travelled to visit the churches. We visited a different church each Sunday. The new VW microbus usually got us to our destination without getting stuck in the deep mud holes.

The congregation at Kwaso is mostly a children's church. They have a student preacher. About eleven young boys, who are members, meet every Sunday and take an active part in the service.

This was the congregation at Anasu. Emanuel Asiama was the fulltime preacher. The average Sunday morning attendance was 12 adults and 25 children. Six have been baptized and one restored. This picture was taken of the VBS held there.

Harry Simons was the preacher of the New Amakon congregation. He supports himself. The church is self-supporting and they

have about 20-25 who attend every Sunday morning. A VBS was recently held there. The average VBS attendance was over 200. This is part of Kumasi.

We walked along this narrow path to visit in the homes of the members who were sick. Diana, Jane Davenport, Janice, Cathy, Harold and John led the way as Debbie, Jane Ann and the brethren follow. Dwayne Davenport took the picture.

One of the preachers baptized someone who had completed several Bible Correspondence Courses.

April 25, 1964

The children were all bedded down for the night. Harold and I were in the bedroom going over the events of the day. Weakened by several recent bouts of malaria, Harold had spent most of the day resting. I sat in a chair by the side of the bed jotting down items to add to the monthly report as he rattled off one event after another.

"Slow down, I can't write that fast!" I stammered as I looked up at his furrowed brow.

As I waited for a reply, a haunting memory squeezed out all of the other thoughts in my mind. The memory of the fund raising venture exhausted me.

"Sweetheart," Harold answered as he cleared his throat, "we need to talk." He reached over, took the pencil out of my hand, looked seriously at me with his unblinking eyes and questioned, "I'm very concerned about you. I can tell how upset you are by your speech," he paused, then he continued, "and you have been stammering a lot these last few weeks. Let's talk about it?"

I looked away surprised by the sudden change in the direction of our conversation. Harold waited for my reply until I regained my composure.

"I suppose that I feel that maybe God will not find the funds for us to get home" I stammered, "and I have been wondering why Ginger was killed so soon. The children try hiding it, but they are devastated." I continued "I'm really anxious about how I will be able to teach Debbie the Sixth Grade Calvert Correspondence School."

Harold quietly responded, "The weak give up and the strong almost do!" His loving eyes met mine. I smiled. We hugged each other tightly. He then turned the conversation back, "Let me tell you a story" he continued as he leaned back and propped up the pillow behind his head. I settled back in my chair and gazed at his understanding eyes as he continued.

"One evening when I was small boy on the farm, my dad brought home a large sack of oysters. While we were all sitting on the back porch shucking oysters, to mother's great delight, my dad found a pearl. When I examined it, I didn't think it was as pretty as the gems in my rock collection.

However as the years have gone by, I learned how pearls were formed. Now pearls are the most beautiful of all precious gems to me. God considers pearls very precious indeed because in Revelation 21:21, the Apostle John describes heaven as a beautiful city with twelve gates and each gate is a pearl. God could have described the gates as rubies or emeralds or diamonds, but he said pearls. Why?

I think God chose pearls because pearls and saints are a great deal alike. They are both the product of a great deal of pain and suffering.

Pearls are formed when a grain of sand or other small foreign material is accidentally trapped in an oyster and causes an irritation. To protect itself, the oyster continually coats the irritant with a special secretion. The result is a pearl. The longer the oyster is left alone, the larger the pearl will grow. The harvest takes place during the late winter months after the oyster has been most active and when the pearls are their most lustrous. So in the attempt to remove pain, the oyster creates a beautiful cocoon around that irritating piece of sand.

We spend most of our life seeking an easy problem-free journey, but God said that his strength is made perfect in weakness, and that when we are weak, then we are strong. God gives us thorns! God says to us just as he said to Paul in 2 Corinthians 12, "My grace is sufficient for you, and my grace is made perfect in weakness." I know how hard you struggle with your speech issues but maybe God gave you this as a thorn to make you strong. I sometimes wonder if this was Paul's thorn because of the hints in the Bible.

Oh, I am sure the oyster tried to get rid of that irritating grain of sand, and probably said, "Oh, how I wish I had never opened my shell! I would give anything to flush that sand out!" But the oyster was unable to do so. Our thorns in the flesh are like that irritating grain of sand, but in due time if we faint not, the process of tolerating the thorn brings us into a greater relationship with God and the process makes us a saint.

Every saint who walks through the pearly gates will bear in his body the marks of Jesus Christ. In the process of this life, we will have been transformed from that irritating ugly piece of sand to a beautiful gem. Through those days of becoming that beautiful gem, we will have borne the bitter pains, heartaches, and disappointment as a disciple of Jesus Christ. Only saints who are willing to bear the thorns in this life will surround God's throne.

Time always decided and divided the real pearls from the imitation. As the years go by, the natural pearl gains in beauty. There is something deep within a pearl that seems to grow more beautiful and lush as the years go by."

With a reassuring smile, he reached over and clasped his hand in mine and gently whispered, "God is making you a real pearl, sweetheart."

Our eyes met. I brushed away a tear and smiled.

"Let's pray about how we can re-arrange our schedule better to give you more time to be alone and rest. I know how much you enjoy reading and meditating. We'll just have to figure out how to make it happen."

I nodded, as he continued, "Think about this now. No one plants olive trees any more because it takes fifty years to get the first crop. Remember that we are planting olive trees."

April 30, 1964

Dear Mother and Daddy,

Yes, Harold is well now. It was malaria. We have changed our diet and are taking more vitamins. We are eating more groundnuts (peanuts) which are high in protein and we are taking iron and extra vitamin C. I'm sorry I didn't write sooner.

I usually write 40-50 letters each month to individuals to try to sustain interest in the work here and hopefully to bear fruit financially. I try to answer all of the letters that we receive. Now I'm 100 letters behind. Usually I wait, let them stack up and when an exciting bit of news happens I make a standard letter and mail the letter to everyone. I am always looking for stories to share.

This is report time and I dread the financial bookwork! We are also gathering materials for a VBS at Suminakese May 4 -8. This is a 2 ½ hour drive one way from Kumasi-a hard drive in the mountains. We have 1,000 little gold crowns with Church of Christ Vacation Bible School (in Twi) to cut out by hand. The girls are helping with this. We have also translated some literature to hand out each day — a memory verse and a picture. This had to be typed on a stencil and mimeographed.

God will bless you for all you are doing to raise funds for the Ghana work. We were very privileged recently to attend a devotional with the Southern Baptist missionaries and to hear discussions with Dr. H. Cornell Goerner, the mission's area representative from Richmond, Virginia. He flew here for a few days to encourage us. His devotional text was Ecclesiastes 11:1-6. He visits all of their missionaries periodically. He reminded us of E.W. McMillan.

It is definite now. No one will replace the Davenports. Continue your prayers.

Love you both very much,
Jane Ann

May 10, 1964

A few days after Harold talked to me about my speech problems, I decided it was time for me to reorganize my hectic schedule and to get back to my daily visits with God. Those visits had pulled me through my horrible ordeal in Santa Ana, California.

Surprisingly, in the barrels, I had found my notes and prayer diary detailing those times –1959 and 1960. As I opened up my prayer journal, the entry dated April 10, 1960 jumped out. We were in Santa Ana, California and I was in the depths of depression. Just a few days before, Harold had been presented a letter from the elders saying that I needed psychiatric and medical help. They stated that my condition was so hopeless that Harold should give up entirely his plans to preach and certainly forget the mission work. I read as much as I could absorb, and quickly turned several pages to a journal dated April 16, 1960.

Today I was again into the depths of depression and despair. I was in the bedroom and Harold and the children were outside. The telephone rang several times. When no one else answered, I picked up the receiver and stammered, "Hello."

"Hello, this is Bob Irby," he said in a very surprised tone of voice. "Do you remember me?" he questioned.

"Yes, you're the preacher from Compton." I replied wondering why he called.

"I heard you were sick and I called to say that we have all been praying for you," he continued in a very concerned voice.

"How did you hear that I was sick?" I stammered.

"It was announced at the Daily Chapel Service at Pepperdine University several times in their prayers," he replied.

"We love you and we are praying for you," he replied with a tone of strong encouragement. His voice softened as he continued, "Cast all your cares on God, for He cares for you." After repeating this several times, he followed with, "Get your Bible and read this over and over again, 1 Peter 5:7, "casting all your care on Him, for He cares for you."

I didn't know how to answer so there was a big silence.

"Just remember we are praying for you. We love you. God Bless. Bye," he then ended the call.

This distant memory triggered another recollection of that following night. As I tried to sleep, this Scripture kept rolling, and then racing around in my mind like a never ending cycle until I was so exhausted that I fell asleep.

This thought jarred me back to my present moment. That was then. This is now and I am sitting in our home in Kumasi, Ghana. With this revelation, I could feel cold chills reverberate throughout my body as I sat in awe, absorbing the power of prayer and God's love for me. So I wrote a poem.

I KNEW NOT THE PATH

My God and I walked through the day,
I knew not the path, but he pointed the way.
At first I was stubborn and lagged behind,
But He patiently waited, while the path I struggled to find.

As a sweet, gentle breeze,
I sought a rose-strewn path of ease.
But storm clouds quickly arose,
And I froze!

The pathway grew black,
And I struggled to go back.
In a maze of pathways, I was hopelessly lost!

Oh, what a terrible cost!
Weeping and praying in dark despair
"Oh, God, do you really care!"

In the blackness of that terrible night,
He graciously restored my sight.
As I opened my Bible and started to pray,
I knew not the path-but he pointed the way.

Debbie, Diana and Janice cut out VBS crowns for the VBS in Suminakese.

This is a picture of a group of Suminakese leaders who attended the VBS everyday. The man in the back holding the child came everyday. He is a Muslim. His child was very sick. We prayed for his child and treated her for malaria.

A group picture of the people who attended the VBS at Suminakese. Everyone enjoyed wearing their crowns.

May 11, 1964

Dear Mother and Daddy,

I know you must wonder why you haven't received any letters. We have been extremely busy and dealing with a lot of problems. The electricity was off for several days. Then the water was off. Next the power was off again. This seems to happen quite often now. We don't know why.

The importation of food is still a problem. Foods are getting scarce and much more expensive. A Ladies Bible Class in Santa Ana sent us a big box of food last week. It was greatly appreciated. They included a two pound box of Old English cheese. We enjoyed it very much. We have no cheese here. Helen Clark and her group keep us in their prayers and constantly send us letters and boxes. Remember we stayed with them quite a while when we were living in the trailer raising funds in California.

The VBS at Suminakese was very successful. We had over 200 enrolled with an average attendance of 114. We had two baptisms. This was the first time a VBS had ever been conducted in this remote mountain village of 1,000. Classes were held in a spacious Catholic Primary School building situated on top of a hill overlooking the town. It was an impressive sight to see many children and 25 adults wearing their Church of Christ VBS crowns, marching up the hill to class every morning at 7:00. Since most of the adults are farmers, they brought their tools and lunches with them to attend the Bible study. After class they walked to their farms and the marketplace wearing their crowns.

Two days ago, the oldest daughter of E.A. Asante, the preacher at Old Tafo, died after suffering many months with an incurable heart condition. When a person dies in the tropics, she must be buried the same day or early the following morning. Embalming is not practiced in Ghana. Great Christian love was shown as the brethren and friends took charge of the situation. They informed all the brethren to come to the Asante home that evening for a special season of prayer. This brought a rich and heartwarming experience to all. As we sang and prayed, we could witness comfort and strength filling the hearts of this family as their entire countenance changed. Later Christians went into the Asante home and dismantled the bed of the little girl and removed all of her personal property, including pictures, after providing food for the family. The funeral expenses are all borne by the church members, friends and relatives.

Early the next morning, Christian friends went to the hospital and collected the body; bathed, clothed and laid the body in a simple wooden box, and carried it to the back of the VW. We slowly drove to the burial grounds. By an unmarked grave, a short service was conducted by Harold and Dwayne. The family was not present. Christians here do not permit a bereaved family to know where their loved one is buried because they know that the bereaved family would want to go there and weep. This would cause much sorrow. Ghanaian Christians know that the body is in the grave but the real person is alive with God because Christ gave us victory over death. We left and went to the Asante home. Harold conducted a short service. Afterwards, they served us refreshments.

When we left the burial grounds, we observed a pagan funeral taking place. People screamed, cried, sobbed and danced. Some of the women were rolling on the ground. Others sat with downcast eyes. Some were consuming enormous amounts of alcohol. What a contrast!

We are very busy making plans for Dwayne and Jane's departure. We're planning a big party for them at our home.

Write soon.

Love,
Jane Ann

May 12, 1964

After we left the funeral, I couldn't stop thinking about the pagan funeral that we had observed, so at our next trip to the library I did some research about Ghanaian pagan funerals and found out that the Ghanaian does not ignore the fact of death. They believe that death is a necessary phase in the perpetual cycle of existence, and that every man is predestined by God to live a certain allotted time for a specific purpose and that sooner or later man will die and return again. The belief in re-incarnation causes them to believe in ancestral worship, and that the spirits of their ancestors come back to live in their children. The spirits of the dead are believed to be going on a journey. Therefore, food, water and all the necessities for a long journey are placed in front of the corpse lying in state. After the burial, the food is moved to the grave site. I am glad that I did the research. It helps me to better understand the people. (Meyerowitz Ghana and Ancient Egypt 186-215)

May 13, 1964

Dear Grandma and Grandpa,

Thank you for your letters and the boxes.

Mommy has been teaching me. The Calvert books came in. I like it because she doesn't teach me every day. Then I have time to read and write letters. We have a wonderful library here. We go every two weeks and get armloads of books.

We have good friends here. They are Baptist missionaries. They have a daughter my age. She is coming home this week from

Nigeria. She attends the Baptist School in Nigeria for missionary children. They have asked me to come to a slumber party next week. A Canadian girl is coming too.

I have a boy friend now. He came to see me Saturday. All my sisters watched from the next room and giggled.

That's all I have to say today.

Yours,
Debbie

May 20, 1964

Here we are again, God. It's just You and me. It is so difficult to find a time for us to be alone, but I am going to keep trying until I find the best time each day because I need You so much. As I read Your Word today, this new thought shouted at me.

Christ had to come to be a real live living example to show me what You are really like. No one has seen You face to face. The human part of me tends to be afraid of the unknown, but You want me to know what a loving, compassionate God You are. That love caused You to develop the plan for Your Son to come to earth to live in a fleshly body and to reveal Your personality to me so I could have the opportunity to view You as a loving, caring and understanding God. As Your Word says, the goodness of God causes me to repent. Afterwards, I will be delighted to savor Your presence as I feast on Your Word and ask Your Holy Spirit to direct my thoughts, lips, and actions. If Christ died for me when I was His enemy, how much more will He help me if I am a seeker of His Will? Thank You, God!

May 25, 1964

I was able to squeeze out a block of time tonight to be with You alone God. With my hectic schedule, I need to revise the schedule I used before. After reviewing some of notes, here is the new schedule that I hope, with Your help will meet my daily challenges.

MY DAILY VISIT WITH GOD

1. Find a quiet place to be completely alone.
2. Decide on a convenient time.
3. Never miss the appointment.
4. Put my Study Bible, Bible Concordance, Prayer Journal and plenty of pencils in a convenient place so I can easily find them.
5. Start my session with a prayer.
6. Read the Bible, with these questions in mind: Are there actions I need to change? What destructive emotion do I need God's help to release? Imagine that Christ is talking to me personally. What do You want me to learn today?
7. Date my prayer journal page.
8. Briefly state my present concerns.
9. Find a Bible passage to address those concerns.
10. Meditate on the Bible passage as I relax my mind and body.
11. Pray that God will open up my eyes to see His answer.
12. Leave plenty of space at the end of that day in the journal to record God's answers.
13. Review past journal entries to re-read about my experiences and how God answered my prayers. Thank God for helping me. I know that focusing on God's help in the past will strengthen my faith that God will help solve any present crisis.

After I reviewed my outline, I thumbed through one of my journals and stopped when I saw a poem that I had written in early 1960 as I was recovering from my miserable illness after the trauma in Santa Ana, California.

THE ANCHOR OF THE SOUL

Loved ones come and loved ones go;
The Word of God abides forever.
Friends come and friends go;
The Word of God lives forever.
Happiness comes and happiness goes;
The Word of God delights forever.
Success comes and success goes;
The Word of God challenges forever.
Fortunes come and fortunes go;
The Word of God provides forever.
Houses come and houses go;
The Word of God stands forever.
Good health comes and good health goes;
The Word of God endures forever.
Memories come and memories fade;
The Word of God lasts forever.
The seasons come and the seasons go;
The Word of God is forever.
Earth and heaven shall vanish away;
The Word of God shall remain forever.

At the end of my poem, I read a statement that I had scribbled: I learned that the key to unlock the door to the Bible Treasure House is prayer.

I left this sacred moment with a firm resolve to make sure that I kept my daily appointments with God.

May 30, 1964

Dear Grandma and Grandpa,

I got your letter today and I am writing back the same day. I'm not sick any more. I think I got sick because I forgot to take my malaria medicine. I'm not surprised. It isn't the first time.

I am so happy here. New things happen every day. John Law, our gardener, night watch and floor mopper, came to the door and showed us that his back hurt. He asked for some of the bitter pills. He thinks the pills have more power if they taste bitter. We gave him some aspirin. He isn't a Christian but we hope he will be some day.

We are getting ready to give a going away party for DDD (short for Davenports). This is Friday and the party is Sunday afternoon after church. We expect about 40 people. Mommy is going to serve donuts. The people here enjoy them so much.

I'm looking forward to spending time with the Baptist missionary girl. She is only eleven and about a year younger than I am but we will still have lots of fun together. She will be home from Nigeria for about three month's for her summer vacation.

Good Bye. Write soon.

Yours in Christ,
Debbie

June 3, 1964

Dear Friends,

The days are passing swiftly and so many jobs are not completed. Davenports left for the States. Now we are the only Church of Christ missionaries in Ghana. Pray for us.

Sunday we had a great fellowship with the brethren here. A special farewell service was conducted for the Davenports after worship. Afterwards, later in the afternoon, we had a farewell party in our home. About 50 brethren came to enjoy homemade donuts and orange soda pop. Many could not speak English and our Twi skills are poor. Yet we were bound together in the bonds of love through Jesus Christ. We spent two enjoyable hours singing together praises to God. Two hours and 150 donuts later, we presented the Davenports a tape of both services. I am sure they will look back with joy many years from now at this wonderful occasion and thank God for blessing their labors here.

Brother Young, who is working with the Akwapim people in Koforidua reported that he plans to baptize five more in a few days. All of these people graduated from the Bible Correspondence Courses. Four Ghanaian preachers plan to hold a VBS there in

August. Enrollments for the Bible Correspondence Courses continue to increase each month. Many more would be baptized if we had workers to travel into the other regions of Ghana to baptize those who request it after completing the courses.

We recently made a color slide taped report of the Ghana work. The adult series is 35 minutes long with 72 pictures. The children's report has 36 pictures and a 10 minute tape narrated by Janice. Contact the Cedars church if you would like to borrow this report to show to your congregation.

Last week John was in the hospital to have some warts cut out under his chin. He had seven stitches. It is healing nicely. Yesterday he started to school.

Jane Ann Derr

*This is a picture of Dewayne and Jane Davenport at the Kumasi
Airport in front of their Ghana Airways plane. They were leaving
Kumasi to return to the United States. We were very sad to see
them go.*

June 8, 1964
Letter from Wendell Broom

Dear Derrs,

Thanks so much for the wonderful slide and tape report. We
showed it to the VBS and they wrote you the attached letter in a
scroll in gratitude for your work for Christ. The report was another

excellent one, getting right to the point we were trying to emphasize. We are very grateful to you for preparing it for us.

Our new building is moving well along. The beams are up and crews are working on the decking. Wiring is going in and heating ducts, with plenty of work yet to be done. Bonds are moving slowly, but moving. About $91,000 sold as of now. We need to sell $50,000 more.

That's all the news from here. Our love to all of you. May your family's welfare hold steady in the turmoil of the Ghanaian upsets. Preach the Word. Pray for us as we do for you.

Wendell Broom

Minister
Cedars Church of Christ
Wilmington, Delaware

June 10, 1964

Today as I worked toward developing a plan for my daily devotional, I reviewed my last journal and reflected on the thought that the key to unlocking the door to the Bible Treasure House is prayer. So I went directly to the Bible and prayed that God would help me understand His plan for me today then patiently waited for the Holy Spirit to direct me. I learned that I became confused if I read what others said the Bible taught and it would only be clear to me if I went to the Bible directly to look for fresh discoveries of God's Truth. This whetted my appetite to want to learn more.

I found it helped me so much to pick a theme, and make a Scripture Bank of that theme. I chose hope as my first theme because I wanted to overcome my fears. Next I picked trusting in God as my second theme.

After writing down all of my Scriptures of each theme, I read these Scriptures into a tape recorder and played the tapes during the day especially when I was fearful and depressed. Next I prayed for a renewed effort to continue my daily prayer journals to keep a record of the Scripture of the day and my foremost problem. Afterwards, I recorded God's answer to my prayers! In the past I found out that the answers came in changing circumstances, a remark from someone, a thought or sometimes a dream or an urge to respond in some way to an action. When God said no to my prayers, sometimes much later I discovered why the answer was no and learned that God was protecting me from some type of harm that I knew nothing about. I learned that God is good and I yearned to thank Him and praise Him daily for His goodness.

I discovered that the Bible itself is a fantastic manifestation of God's love, patience, and care for us and is full of hidden treasures. I found that if I searched with a lazy, half-hearted purpose I would not find the treasure, but if I really took the time to ransack the Bible, I was richly rewarded.

June 15, 1964

Harold is building another model Mercy Ship. He just won't give up. The Mercy Project actually started and was born while we were both in the depths of despair in Santa Ana, California in 1959 and 1960. After our dreams of going to New Zealand as missionaries were shattered, Harold enrolled as a student at Pepperdine University.

While he was there he met another student Isong Ibok-Ete. Isong was a dynamic, likeable, kind Nigerian, who was constantly recruiting and pleading for Christians to go to Nigeria. He spoke often for desperately needed doctors to go as medical missionaries.

Shortly after, Harold met John Westland, a great Christian and a former Navy man. In Harold's mind, the idea soon blossomed of taking a hospital ship with medical missionaries to places where the gospel and health care was not presently available.

Remembering this sparked a thought. People come into our lives like shooting stars — here for a moment, then gone. God sends them for a purpose, and then they leave. They are bright lights and soon they fade away. These bright lights turned the tide in Harold when he was so depressed about our New Zealand missionary plans and my devastating illness. A spark was ignited and Harold quickly emerged from his heartbreaking moments and started to build a model ship and a medical evangelism display. He was elated when he found out that the church could buy a World War Two LST ship for a very small price, and he figured out how it could easily be converted to a floating hospital.

Almost instantly our present circumstances changed. Harold's mother, Susie Derr flew from Terre Haute, Indiana to our rundown house in Santa Ana. Our house had been provided by one of the members rent free. It was one of her rental houses that had been condemned and she allowed us to live there temporarily until the house could be torn down. Before I could catch my breath, Susie Derr had packed up all of our things, Harold had rented a U-Haul trailer, and we were all on our way to Terre Haute, Indiana.

Once we were in Indiana, the house across the street from Harold's parents became available, and his parents arranged for us to buy the house. Immediately, Harold started working for his Dad in the family ornamental iron business. Harold and his Dad had started the business when Harold was in high school. The shop stood on a site that had been an ironworker's factory in 1793. The shop started out with blacksmithing, and later developed into the making of wagons and buggies, and Harold bragged about finding blueprints for wagon wheels for a cannon used during the Civil War. As a teenager, Harold had served as a wheelwright under an eighty-six-year-old man. So Harold felt comfortable returning to the shop to help his Dad. He thought it was a mixed blessing as he considered this move would dash to pieces his dream of mission work.

However, after several months of calmly catching our breath, absorbing the comfortable feelings of our familiar roots and loving memories of our courtship and marriage, a shocking discovery was made. The church on the south side of town needed a preacher. Harold talked to me about this opportunity and then applied, and was accepted.

Very shortly, Harold met a very unusual couple Earl and Mabel Petty. Earl was a most remarkable person. He was an elderly retired State Department official and his job had been to allocate surplus equipment and material. He was a personal friend of Averill Harriman and General Rampy and was at the Malta Conference with Franklin Roosevelt and Stalin. Earl immediately loved the challenge and saw the need of this medical missionary ship project. He agreed to organize a non-profit organization for this project to be accomplished and also to be the corporate secretary. The name Mercy was then chosen.

In the two years that followed, Harold developed a beautiful model ship display and I made a silk banner with the name Mercy outstretched across the world. He then presented the project to several churches, and was a speaker several times at Michigan Christian College at lectureships where additional interest was established. Great encouragement was given by many missionaries, including a host of Nigerian missionaries and several doctors liked the idea, especially a man named Henry Farrar.

In January 1963 Harold decided to resign as preacher for the McKeen Street Congregation in Terre Haute and to spend all his time trying to find a sponsoring church and to find funds for us to go to Nigeria. He went to another lectureship at Michigan Christian College to find support. I stayed home with the children to try to sell the house. He got the sponsor and I sold the house. By May we had purchased a 17 foot trailer and then we embarked on our four and a half month's 5,700 mile fund raising journey.

Now we are here in Ghana, and I am trying to see what purpose God has for us now. As my mind wanders, I try to remember all of the pieces of our experiences. Our zigzagged pattern of events that makes up our strange patchwork puzzle, just doesn't make sense to me. I am trying to put the pieces together and I am confused. *God I need your help!*

This is a picture of the model Mercy Ship that Harold used when he presented the medical mission challenge at Michigan Christian College near Rochester, Michigan in 1961.

This is a picture of the banner that Jane Ann made for the Mercy Ship display at Michigan Christian College.

June 18, 1964

Dear Mother and Daddy,

Thank you for the music tape with your message at the end. Harold is still in the process of building another model ship. This one will be made of tin and naturally will be bigger and better than the first.

I am attaching another list of prospective churches for you to contact.

In April I mentioned that the women in Anansu were attempting to build their own meeting place, but lacked sufficient money for the roof. We had asked for prayers for them. As a result $429 was given to assist them in completing this building. Recently two of the women lost children but they are continuing to forge ahead with this project. One little baby died unexpectedly and the other little boy five died with measles. Now the church has a fulltime preacher.

Yesterday I gave a birthday party for Cathy. Twelve little girls came. A French girl's mother made Cathy a dress. It is so pretty. I'll use your money to buy Cathy new shoes.

Janice has been very sick with an ear infection. She is better now. John likes school very much but is disappointed that he doesn't have enough work to do. He is very anxious to learn. In our morning devotions, he is usually the first one to pop up with the right answer. He has informed us that he wants a British haircut. He does not want any more crew cuts or flat tops. He will probably be put up to Class 2 in September.

I must close. Will write more very soon.

Love,
Jane Ann

This picture was taken at Cathy's birthday party. In addition to Diana, Debbie, Janice, Cathy and John, the guests were all class-mates at Ridge School. Cathy is peeking out from the back of the group.

June 20, 1964

In my devotional today this thought popped up: Living by the Holy Spirit is like Peter walking on the water. As long as I focus on Christ, the Holy Spirit is available, but if I waver and focus else-where, the power leaves, and I sink and fall like Peter. *God I need Your help every second!*

June 29, 1964

Dear Grandma and Grandpa,

I got your very nice letter yesterday and I'm answering it today. This is Sunday afternoon. We had American imported fried chicken for dinner. Believe me, there wasn't any left on the platter. John and Janice even tried to eat the bones. We can't eat the fried chicken from here because it is so tough. Daddy is considering getting some baby chicks, fencing them, and feeding them corn. So maybe they will be tender so we can fry them.

Janice and Diana both share the same room. Their school is scheduling a play to raise funds for the school. Janice got the leading part as Snow White. She will be practicing all summer for the part.

At church this morning the cutest little girl about two or three years old walked in through the front door and instantly sat down between Daddy and Diana. She sat quietly all through the worship service.

Lots of Love,
Yours in Him,
Debbie

June 30, 1964

God, today my devotional is going to have to consist of random thoughts and prayers as I type up the stencils for the Ghana Bible College lessons. Bless our children. They are having a very difficult time grieving over the loss of Ginger and Nutmeg. Thank you, God, for helping us to find two beautiful grey parrots. Maybe the children can concentrate now on teaching the parrots to talk.

Wednesday, July 1, 1964

Dear Mother and Daddy,

We must delay again sending you the tape. It is quite complicated to make a tape here. The power has to be just right. The power is off at night most of the time. Sometimes heavy rains start and you can't hear. Other times workers constantly interrupt. We enjoy your tape very much.

Cedars VBS sent us a letter scroll. They took a piece of wide white paper about 8 to 10 feet long and each class wrote a message on the scroll with magic marker and everyone signed their names. We enjoyed it very much.

How are you coming along showing the Ghana slides? I believe you will find that patience and persistence eventually win out. Thank you so much.

When importation stopped, that included Bibles, too. The Presbyterians, who publish the Twi Bible, have stopped printing them now. Our washer broke yesterday. Our refrigerator sounds as if it is ready to stop. Little Jerry threw something in the toilet and stopped it up big time. We went all over Kumasi trying to buy a plunger. Everyone laughed. There are none in Ghana for sale. Harold rigged up a devise to help by using our garden hose and forcing water through it real fast. The Lord helped us on the washer. We found the belt we needed. One store had a few for their own personal use but decided to let us have one.

The Baptist mission here has five families and two single girls. They are planning a pitch-in picnic for a July 4 celebration and included us! We expect 15 adults and 17 children. Everyone is going to dig into their imported food cabinets and have a real American picnic. We are so looking forward to it. They are so special to us and include us in most all of their socials and devotionals. Most of the Baptists brought over food and household effects to last for their entire tour.

Harold is very busy building the model ship…another LST. This one is about 8 – 10 feet long and made out of metal. This one will be remote controlled and have workable parts. It really gives him a great diversion from the constant problems of the mission and then he is able to see things more clearly.

He is working on the curriculum for the Bible College. It really never had one. Glenn Martin sent the one from Ukpom Bible College in Nigeria. He sent many excellent suggestions which Harold is trying to incorporate for here. He is trying to increase the classes from six hours per week to eighteen hours per week plus he has given each student a definite schedule for other week's activities. All of the preachers must turn in a weekly station report now. All must do a specified number of jobs during the week. Harold is trying to work it out so that we issue each preacher the material that we feel he should have for Bible classes. He is also painting "Church of Christ Meets Here" signs for all the congregations. Then we are working on textbooks for the college. I am typing up a LOT of stencils for these classes and then we will need a lot more. You might mention in your talks that if any congregation would have adult workbooks (as many as five to six copies of each used book) that are just laying around gathering dust, we would be very happy to put them to good use. We could also use any other Christ-centered books.

I must close. Will write more soon.

Love,
Jane Ann

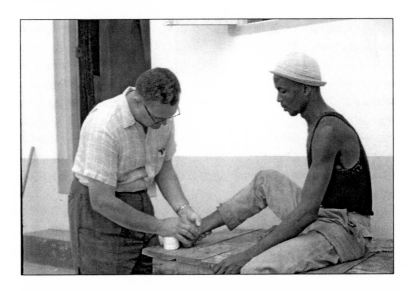

Behind our house is a small building that contains our offices, a classroom for the Bible Training School, Bible Correspondence Office, and a small dispensary. Many sick people came to be treated. We stocked some first aid supplies. The Muslim young man came to us with a guinea worm in his foot. These worms embed themselves in the bottom of the foot and after entering the flesh, develop into a small size worm. This may be as big around as spaghetti and as long as five feet. If untreated, the worm will work its way to the muscle tissue up through the leg and come out where Harold's finger is—just below the knee. If medication is applied to the place where the worm entered the foot, this forces the worm to retract. When

the worm sticks its head out the hole, a small string is tied around the worm and then tied to a small match stick. Afterward, we very carefully and slowly, wind the worm around the stick at the rate of about an inch every four to five days. Guinea worms are found in the drinking water and when ingested begin growing just under the skin. They are extremely painful and often cripple the carrier.

Guinea worms, along with malaria and dysentery were very prevalent. With our limited experience, knowledge and supplies, we just did what we could to relieve pain. They seemed happy that we had taken the time to listen to their problems and to pray with them.

July 9, 1964

Dear Mother and Daddy,

I haven't had time to write. I am spending most of my time typing the stencils for urgently needed textbooks for the Bible Training School.

Our tape recorder is broken. We need a new belt. The stores do not have any belts.

We bought two grey parrots. The children enjoy them immensely.

We are all well except Harold. He has a bad cold. This is the rainy season.

We are thankful you were able to get the appointments to show the Ghana film. We are praying that many will give to help the Ghana work.

Love,
Jane Ann

July 12, 1964

It looks like my journals now will consist mostly of my collection of Scriptures on hope. I am picking one or two a day and I am trying to focus on them every time I get discouraged. Today, I discovered that some of the definitions of hope mean trusting, patient endurance and joyful assurance of God's salvation. *God I need Your help!*

July 16, 1964

Dear Mother and Daddy,

We received your letter today about the disappointing results from El Cajon Boulevard. Don't be discouraged. We are still getting money from churches that we thought would never give. That was a good place for you to practice. You are finding out fast about raising funds.

You mentioned Sister Wagner and the area-wide ladies meeting. By all means, make that appointment. Widows and very poor people supported us until Cedars in Wilmington took over our salary in September. From May to September those dear saints supported us with prayers and their financial support. Never underestimate the power of one individual.

This ladies group is a prayer group that helps missionaries. They have mailed us two boxes of food and write to us. They also sent $25 for the Anansu church building. They are very interested in the Ghana work. Helen Clark is a member of this group. She was the one who invited us to spend several weeks in their home when we were so desperate in Santa Ana. This ladies group is a wonderful group.

Thanks again for your help. God bless.

Love,
Jane Ann

July 27, 1964

Dear Grandpa and Grandma,

We got your tape and were so happy to hear Walt Disney songs. We hadn't received any mail for a long time. Yesterday we hit the jackpot and got lots of mail. It was so good hearing from you.

We got two grey parrots recently. It is fun watching them eat. They eat palm nuts, sugar cane, corn and sand.

We are out of school until September 7. Just six weeks, and I can hardly wait. Debbie's Calvert books came so she is in school now. I can't wait to take Calvert. Her Lorna Doone book looks so interesting. Mother and Daddy are going to pull me out of school in September.

Bye!

Love,
Diana Lynn

July 29, 1964

Dear Mother and Daddy,

I am getting so behind with letter writing. Time slips by and I only accomplish a few items on my jobs to do list. I'm swamped typing stencils for the Bible Training School. I have a Twi Bible Tract waiting to be typed, and **must** be mimeographed by Friday morning. We are composing a Twi songbook with 150 songs in Twi with English words under the Twi. Now we have a songbook with 50 Twi songs and the missionaries cannot sing "in the spirit and understanding".

I do feel so relieved that I just got the July Report completed. It is ready to be mailed. The financial report is always a great challenge. Most of the expenses here are paid 25 to 50 cents at a time for lorry fares for preachers, kerosene and glass for tilley lanterns, small hardware and parts to repair mission equipment. If a missionary does not keep accurate records, he could soon get his personal bank account in a very sad condition. I so wish I had an adding machine.

Ridge School is out for the summer vacation until September 7. Debbie's Calvert books are in. I couldn't get started on her school because I had to get the Ghana Reports out, make the payroll for the preachers, and the girls gave a farewell party for one of their school friends. I feel so guilty for not being able to spend more time on Debbie's school.

I think we are going to let Comfort go and get a fulltime licensed steward. Comfort does a great job however she is able to work only mornings. She has a little baby and two other small children to care for. We feel very sad about this, but I need relief immediately to be able to take care of all of my urgent jobs. Pray for us!

I cannot send you a tape. The recorder is broken and we cannot get parts. Our friend in Accra is trying to get us the part. We are so thankful that you got Ghana funds from Allied Gardens Congregation. Attached is another updated contact list that needs follow-up.

Prices here continue to increase as the shortages become greater. Auto parts are extremely difficult to find such as tires, spark plugs, brakes and batteries. We have been going to Accra for supplies. Since gasoline is so expensive, our car expenses have increased drastically.

The Ghana newspaper reports that the Ghana Government is considering devaluating the Ghana pound, and is also placing greater restrictions on imports. Ghana's economy is based on cocoa. They have recently discovered large areas of diseased trees that they must destroy. Also the world market price on cocoa is decreasing rapidly. Ghana is in a very critical financial situation.

The only way anyone is able to leave Ghana now is to pay for their airline ticket with American dollars or English pound sterling. A new law was just passed stating that any self-employed person cannot take or send his money outside of Ghana. The newspaper said that people leaving Ghana can only take out one suitcase. So far this has not applied to missionaries but only to merchants and self-employed.

Another complication to our work is the big push the Ghana Government is making to unite the main denominational religious groups into one national unified church. They have been working on this since 1957, and it now looks as if they will launch this effort next year. If this happens, it is a case of join or leave. We cannot join. Under the unified program, all church properties come under the jurisdiction of the unified committee. This means that any building the brethren have built, they will lose. In addition, they will not offi-cially be able to gather for worship service.

In May the Baptists lost their big high school valued over a million dollars. The government just came in and took over. They have a seminary just outside of Kumasi, which the government has threat-ened to take. They also operate a large hospital in Northern Ghana and it seems only a matter of time until the Ghana Government take that also. The Baptists spend $50,000 a month in Ghana. They have already officially informed the Unified Church Committee that they will not join or participate in their activities. The Salvation Army and Assemblies of God have also declined to join. Our effort here is so small that no one has contacted us. We are trying to be as inconspicuous as possible.

This presents a tremendous challenge to us. The people are so eager to hear the message of Jesus Christ. We must do everything we are able to do now to strengthen the brethren for what we perceive as their bleak future. Comfort and BO assure us that God will provide.

Thanks again for helping us. We pray many will respond and give generously as you present the Ghana films. Jimmy Lovell printed Harold's report of the work here in the May issue of Action. He also sent us $200 to print the Bible Correspondence Courses. I don't think he realizes how much his " Miss a Meal Campaign" impacts the lives of missionaries.

Love,
Jane Ann

August 10, 1964

During my devotional today, as I picked up the prayer journal I had written on our fund raising trip, a letter fell to the floor. When I peeked inside the letter, tears started to trickle down my cheeks onto the letter as I read, "Please forgive me for being part of a plan to sabotage your New Zealand missionary efforts. Later, I found out that everything I was told was a lie. Please forgive me." This letter came from one of our former co-workers.

My mind returned to that dark depressing time. May 1, 1959, Harold had resigned as Supervisor of the Ballistic Missile Laboratory at Edwards Air Force Base, California. He had served as a liaison officer between the government and private industry while supervising the testing of Ballistic Missiles including the Atlas and the Thor. He worked through all of these challenges, while also launching a preaching career at a mission church in Boron. The Lord had blessed his efforts. Harold loved the challenge and the excitement of witnessing first hand the transforming power of the Holy Spirit into the lives of people.

When an opportunity to be involved in mission work in New Zealand developed, Harold eagerly pursued this. He was able to land the funds, and find a sponsoring congregation. We sold our home and furniture, packed barrels for New Zealand, and moved to Santa Ana where we then expected to sail on the SS Orsava ship September 7, 1959.

Some of our disgruntled co-workers, who couldn't easily find their support, told lies about us and then the sponsoring church refused to send us.

After Harold resigned from a promising career, and we had disrupted our entire life, I could not cope with all the anger, hurt, and disappointment, five small children, living around strangers, and going from the desert to a large metropolitan area. I went into a deep depression. I stayed in our dark bedroom and cried for days on end. Every day seemed worse than the day before and I had no idea how we would survive.

Today, as I looked around my surroundings in Ghana, West Africa, I stopped and tearfully thanked God for sending us here. I started thinking of all the precious saints we had met and the wonderful lessons we had learned in Ghana. I prayed that God would forgive all who had plotted against us knowing that God had used all of these experiences to lead us to Ghana. Then this thought led me to a stronger feeling of God's providential care and knowledge that He would guide us now in our many challenges.

Sunday August 16, 1964

Dear Mother and Daddy,

The children are out of school and everywhere is a buzz of activity. The Bible College is out on vacation and the ten preachers are back in their villages preaching. The girls are filling in and helping grade the Bible Correspondence Courses. Many letters come in everyday.

The girls and I have been sewing. They need school clothes. We bought plenty of fabric at the local market. I supervise, cut out the patterns and the girls sew their own garments. They do a great job and are so proud that they can do it themselves.

Harold is spending his time repairing broken and neglected items. He mounted two lights inside our clothes rack. This is the rainy season, and all of his slacks were moldy and mildewy. We hope the lights solve this problem. His next project is to repair a bookcase for the living room with built in lights. He needs to bring his books inside. They are now in the office in the back and are being eaten by little ants and are green with mold.

In spite of the confusion, Debbie and I are progressing with her school. We are on Lesson 10 now. We are having the most trouble with arithmetic and geography. All of the courses are written in a very interesting way. When we are finished, we will both have learned much. The other subjects we have are: Builders of the Old World; Grammar; Reading for Meaning; Reading Skill Builder; Literature; Lorna Doone; Theras and His Town; Swiss Family Robinson and a study of poetry; Spelling; Science; Drawing; and a Child's History of Art and Sculpture. We both enjoy school very much. Diana can't wait until she can start on Calvert. She will probably start in January.

You have really been busy showing the Ghana films. We are glad that you like the Children's Series. Don't wear yourself out with too many appointments. You would be doing a tremendous amount of good if you would just carry on a mailing service for the film. Our prayers are with you. How would you like to know that your daily bread came from raising funds? Ha! Ha!

We have a new problem here. Communion wine is used because Ghana has no grape juice. There are no grapes grown here. All communion wine is imported. We have been told by the merchants that no more will be imported. We have a month's supply now. The Ghana made sweet red wine is a sugar wine made from pineapple juice. Harold has written Cedars a letter asking for their advice as to how to handle this problem.

A brother in the church works for the Agricultural Station here. Harold is working with him to see if the soil conditions here and the climate here would be conducive to growing grapes. Harold pounds out his frustrations working on the model boat and the many repairs, and I pound out my frustrations on the typewriter.

Do you remember our visit to the museum at Balboa Park where we saw all the gadgets natives invented because of necessity? Before this tour is over, we may need to be inventors. We are working through adjusting to the food situation and our food tastes are changing.

Cathy said that she dreamed last night that she was with Grandma at the toy store. The hardest part of the children's adjustment here is dealing with missing the grandparents.

Love,
Jane Ann

August 25, 1964

Dear Grandpa and Grandma,
Thank you for your letter. We enjoyed it very much. Are you still working in the toy store? Janice and I have work also. It is work that you wouldn't think a person our age could do. We read the Bible Correspondence letters, grade lessons, and send tracts and notes. Today Janice and I worked two hours each. There are a lot of letters! Every time we go to the Post Office the box is full of correspondence.

I am beginning to wear Debbie's outgrown clothes now. Mother says that I am growing. She says that I am getting taller but also a lot thinner.

It is the rainy season now and a little bit cooler. It is a big change from the dry season.

School is still out. We go back September 7. Deborah likes her Calvert and I am beginning to wish I had Calvert. I like being out of school. In four months I will be too old to go to Ridge School and Mother will be teaching me Calvert then.

Mother ordered a Bible play book so we could entertain them. The books came in and look very interesting. The books are called,

"Women in Jesus Time", and "People in Jesus Time". I think we had better start now practicing to perform our first play.

We are so happy that you liked the Children's Ghana Film Series.

Love Always,
Diana Lynn

August 27, 1964

Dear Grandma and Grandpa,

Right now I am making Christmas presents. Christmas isn't very far away. Our school is having a summer holiday. Only one more week and we start back to school. We are planning to go to Accra and spend two or three days before school starts.

Do you have fun working in the toy store? I think it would be fun. Did you go to the Rose Parade? I can remember how much fun it was when our entire family went. It was so beautiful.

I had better hurry so I can help prepare lunch. A person next to us is building a new house. Now all we hear is bang, bang, bang and singing! Daddy is really coming along with the model boat. He is going to have furniture. We are making the beds and covering them.

Bye,

Love,
Janice

August 31, 1964

Dear Mother and Daddy,

Many activities have prevented me from having a quiet moment to write. Debbie and I are on Lesson 15 now. It has been easier to teach since we hired the fulltime steward. He is from Upper Volta and a very hard worker. He last worked at the American Embassy in Accra until several families moved back to America. There are plenty of stewards available for work now because so many white people have left Ghana. Now I have had more time to work with Debbie on the schooling and to do office work.

Daddy, I am including the following information about the work here so you can include it in your fund raising presentations.

WE END OUR FIRST YEAR IN GHANA

Bible Correspondence Work

Thousands have enrolled and 958 have graduated successfully. Outside of Ghana, enrollments have been received from Volta Region, Togo, Nigeria, Liberia, Ivory Coast and Cameroons. Three of the student preachers were baptized after completing the course, and later decided to preach. The man who reprints the lessons is studying with one of the native preachers. Five were baptized in Koforidua as a direct result of the courses. A preaching student, who is supporting himself, graduated from the course and decided to attend the training school. Gospel Press has supplied us with many contacts.

Native Preacher Statistics

Four fulltime preachers work with congregations in Old Tafo, Anansu, Koforidua, and one preacher is starting a work in the heart of Kumasi. Two preachers receive partial support from their congregations (Old Tafo and Anansu). Four self-supporting preachers work at Amakom, Suminakese and Old Tafo. Six students are training to preach. One is self-supporting. Three students are able to preach regularly and already have a congregation to work with. Three students still need more training before they will be able to assume a preaching station. The preachers have held twelve gospel meetings and baptized 63.

Nine Congregations Now Meeting Faithfully

1. OWOROBONG Although this town is only 107 miles from Kumasi, it takes 5-6 hours to go there. About ten

members live at the end of the 40 mile bush road. They have no preacher, but Brother Young reports that they are very faithful to meet each Sunday and to observe the Lord's Supper.

2. SUMINAKESE They own their own building, have their own preacher, and are completely self-supporting. About 35 members attend on Sunday mornings. We held a VBS there in May and the average attendance was 114 and many of these were adults.

3. NEW AMAKOM Harry Simons is the preacher. He supports himself. The church is self-supporting. About 20-25 attend Sunday mornings. VBS was held in September with an average attendance of 200. This is part of Kumasi.

4. OLD TAFO This is also part of Kumasi. E. Asante is the preacher. Two of the leaders are capable preachers who go to various congregations to conduct services. They are a self-supporting congregation providing half of their preacher's salary. A VBS was held there in February which resulted in an average attendance of 150. About 20-25 attend on Sunday mornings.

5. ANANSU Emmanuel Asiama is the fulltime preacher. The average Sunday morning attendance is 12 adults and 25 children. Six have been baptized in August and one was restored. VBS is now in progress. They are planning to have their new building completed very soon. They partially support their preacher.

6. SENFIE This is the newest congregation. One of the student preachers works with them three days a week. About 15 attend on Sundays and most are adults. Some members travel and cannot come every week. The meet in the Court House. Two gospel meetings have been held there.

7. KWASO This is a children's church. They have a student preacher. About 11 young boys, who are members, meet every Sunday and take an active part in the services. Many children come.

8. NYAME YENI this is a long, hard drive from Kumasi. They have no preacher. About 2 adults and 6 to 7 boys who are members meet every Sunday.
9. KOFORIDUA Samuel Young was sent as a missionary to Koforidua in December. It is a four hour drive from Kumasi. The results have been very encouraging. Ten members meet each Sunday. This is the only work we have among the Akwapim people. The other work is among the Ashanti.

During the three years of the Ghana work, many congregations have started and many have fallen away. We are sad about this, but it has stirred in our hearts a deeper conviction of the importance of training preachers. Most of the congregations that have fallen away did not have a preacher or only had one occasionally. Through these sad experiences we have learned that it is not practical to start a new congregation until a well trained preacher is able to work with them.

I hope this better helps to understand the work here. Will write more soon.

Love,
Jane Ann

Harold treated people from the back of the VW Microbus. Harold built a small cabinet in the back of the microbus to carry simple medicines and first aid supplies. Very few people in Ghana knew what it felt like to feel well and pain free. Ignorance and super- stition ran rampant. The fetish priest and witch doctor were still very powerful and add to the miseries of the people. They were so appreciative that we took the time to listen to their troubles even if we could not help them.

Jane Ann passed out chewing gum to the children, while Harold answered Bible questions from the adults and treated their physical illnesses. This particular day, Jane Ann had a five cent package of chewing gum from our Christmas boxes from America. She tore each stick of gum into about six pieces and gave each of the chil- dren a piece. We would have never believed that so many children could be so happy over a five cent package of gum. In fact, when we returned the next time, the children showed us their gum.

September 5, 1964

In the middle of the night, after a very stressful, confusing day, we were abruptly awakened by loud screams. Harold and I rushed toward the commotion to discover the problem. Cathy was sitting up in bed stunned. She had just woke up from a terrible nightmare.

"What's wrong sweetheart?" Harold questioned, as he sat on the side of the bed.

"Daddy, I dreamed the soldiers were coming in to kill us!" she sobbed as she wiped a tear from her eye.

"Daddy, Mommy, I'm scared!" said John as he ran to sit on my lap. I gave John a reassuring hug as I listened to Cathy untangle the events of her dream.

Harold sat quietly listening, and then opened up the conversation, "Let me tell you a story," he continued as he gently held her hand and gazed at her frightened face, "When I was a little boy, I didn't have any grandparents. So I adopted an older couple in our neighborhood as my grandparents. They always welcomed me into their home any time and always kept a pan of bread pudding in the warming oven just for me. Every time I walked into their living room, I could see a large picture over the fireplace. It was a beautiful picture of two children, a little boy and a little girl, who were very frightened as they walked across a broken swinging bridge during a storm. A beautiful angel was right behind the children protecting them from harm. Grandma always told me that God sends angels to protect His little children."

Cathy reached over and gave Harold a hug. We had a prayer and then went back to bed.

September 8, 1964

Dear Mother and Daddy,

Debbie and I are doing much better with the school. She is excited. We are going to a movie tonight. Most of the movies are Indian films. All of the singing is very high and we can't understand a word. During the movies the Ghanaians are very noisy, shouting and laughing during a love scene or a good fight. We have learned to imagine our own words. At times the power goes off, the film breaks, or they cut out the main plot.

Our steward is Muslim and last night when Debbie was helping him with the dishes, he asked her about the church. He is always

very interested when we have our morning devotions before breakfast and has been coming through the room for water during this
time. He has to carry hot water from the bathroom to the kitchen
to do the dishes. We think he is very curious. I gave him malaria
medicine and he was very appreciative. It would be wonderful if
he becomes a Christian. He is from Upper Volta and we have no
churches in that African country.

I am including the following article that Harold sent to the
Christian Chronicle. He wanted you to read it from us and not the
paper.

ECONOMIC TURMOIL HINDERS GHANA WORK

September 8, 1964

The spread of the Gospel in Ghana has been greatly hindered the
last few months due to an increasing shortage of supplies, and an
increasing cost of living.

Like all newly independent African nations, Ghana has many
growing pains. The most pressing problem besieging Ghana today
is her poor economy. Her main export is cocoa, and in the last few
years the world market price for cocoa has declined considerably.

To add to this perplexing situation, many of the cocoa trees are
now diseased and must be cut down. It takes a new tree seven to
eight years to start producing cocoa after it is planted.

There are no other main exports to rely on at this time, as it is a
new developing country. Her other main export is lumber, and she
has many competitors in this world market. So with no apparent solu-
tion to these critical problems in sight, it appears that this economic
condition will continue to plague the work here.

ALL IMPORTATION OF GOODS HIGHLY RESTRICTED

All importation of goods to Ghana has been highly restricted
since January of this year. A few things have been imported since
that time. But these imported goods could fill only a small percentage
of the demand. Since the Derr's have arrived in Ghana, September

1963, prices have continued to steadily increase until products now cost twice as much as they did a year ago—when you are fortunate to find these products.

NO FLOUR AVAILABLE....BAKERIES CLOSED

Today no flour is available in Ghana. The bakeries have closed down. It is a strange feeling to see empty bread racks in all of the stores.

The Ghanaians have no facilities to bake bread in their homes. They cook outside on a small charcoal stove; therefore, they depend heavily on the local bakeries for all of their bread. The people are suffering! Ordinary rock salt has increased from one pence to seven pence for the same amount. Cube sugar now sells for a penny a cube.

Many factories have closed down because they cannot get the materials they need to operate or because equipment is broken and they cannot import the needed parts to repair the equipment. Some stores in downtown Kumasi have closed their doors because they cannot import merchandise to sell. Consequently, unemployment is high, and burglary and petty theft is increasing.

NO IMPORTATION OF BIBLES

Until recently, it was fairly easy to buy an inexpensive Bible here. However, now, because of economic conditions, booksellers cannot get a license to import Bibles. We purchase our Bibles from the Bible Society of West Africa. They have informed us that they are no longer able to import Bibles. We may, however, receive Bibles, duty free if they are sent in as a gift, and plainly marked "Gift of Bibles".

BIBLE TRAINING SCHOOL MUST FIND A NEW HOME

Presently, the Bible Training School is meeting in a vacant unfinished house next door to our home. It is owned by our landlord and he has let us use this building rent free. Now he wants to complete this house, and we must find other facilities.

Four students live together in one room upstairs. There is no glass in the windows, and every time it rains, water blows in on the beds. The classroom is downstairs and is very drafty.

Many other suitable houses are available because so many Europeans have left Ghana. However, because of insufficient funds and very high rents, we are not able to move at this time. Our dollars go only half as far as they did when we first came to Ghana a year ago. More students would come to school if we could provide them with $11.20 per month. At present we have five students.

Pray for the church in Ghana. Special prayers are requested in our time of need. Many trials fall upon us daily. We especially need your prayers for wisdom, guidance, and strength.

Hope this report helps with the fundraising. We were able to get the flour we needed yesterday—by the grace of God—at the government wholesale house. We will keep you posted on the work. We are very, very grateful for your help. We are all well at this time.

Love,
Jane Ann

September 15, 1964

I sat on the couch looking out the window, pondering our present dilemma of trying to find the necessary food and supplies for the day. I strained my eyes, hoping to see the familiar sight of the VW Bus and Harold's return from scouting the area for supplies.

My thoughts were abruptly interrupted. "Mommy, read me a story," John insisted as he put the book in my lap and then proceeded to climb on the couch and snuggle beside me.

As I looked at his pleading expression, I couldn't say no. "All right, sweetheart, what story do you want to read?" I said as I thumbed through the pages of "Mrs. Lee's Stories About Jesus."

"Mommy, read the story about Jesus taking the five loaves of bread and two fishes and feeding the people," John quickly answered as he found the story for me.

"Let's see where" I replied.

John interrupted with, "Cathy read me this story last night and I want to hear it again."

"This story comes from the Bible in Matthew 14:13-23," I started out with warm tears trickling down my cheeks and with stammering lips.

John came back with, "Mommy, let me tell you the story."

After John recounted the story he questioned, "Mommy, do you think that Jesus will find us food like He did those people?"

I looked at the innocent, bewildering expression on his face, held him very tightly and replied, "Yes, sweetheart, God and Jesus will provide for us, too!"

Suddenly Harold barged in the front door and said, "What's going on? Will you two come outside and help me unload the VW? I arrived at the stores just as they were restocking. They said the ship finally came in."

Thank You God, for teaching me to trust You when I'm afraid!

September 16, 1964

Dear Mother and Daddy,

The Bible Training School has been discontinued because we have been asked to move. Presently, it is meeting in a vacant unfinished house next door to us. The landlord is now going to finish it. We have no money to rent other facilities.

Harold is writing to the Elders at Cedars. He is asking if he can go back to the States by himself, to raise funds for supporting the work, and to bring back food and supplies for us. The children and I will stay here until he returns. We can carry on the work the best we can.

We were able to get the flour we needed yesterday—by the grace of God—at the government wholesale house.

We will keep you posted. We are very, very grateful for your help.

Love,
Jane Ann

September 20, 1964

Dear Grandma and Grandpa,

It has been raining here all of the time. Sometimes at night, it gets cold and we have to get covers over us. Mommy is still teaching me at home.

I want to send you a little article that I just read in the local paper. The title was MAN DIES AFTER VISITING HIS WIFE. A happy father visited his wife and their new baby at the Maternity Ward of the Kumasi General Hospital yesterday. He told her of the arrangements being made to receive her and her baby at home. But minutes later the father was found dying outside the hospital after he had dived head long into the sidewalk from the 5th floor of the hospital. He was rushed to the casualty ward where he died fifteen minutes later.

This is one of the articles that we read in the paper here everyday. They do have a few good things in the paper. They do have a section devoted to the funnies. The best one tells about their daily life.

Have you heard about the Beatles? Well, I have and I think they are great. I have lots of pictures of them. Sometimes I can hear them sing on the radio. We listen to people talk and sing from about every country. I like to hear them talking and singing in different languages.

Lots of Love,
Debbie Kay

September 26, 1964

It had been a very stressful day. As we were all eating our evening meal, John spoke up, "Daddy, why did you want to be a missionary?"

Stunned by the questions, Harold slowly responded with, "Well, I suppose because of my Bible School teacher when I was a small boy."

"What did she say?" Diana chimed in.

"Yes, tell us Daddy," Janice enthusiastically questioned.

Harold scratched his head, cleared his throat and gazed out the window as if he was sifting through his mind to find the right words. He looked around the table and replied, "She made it sound like it would be such an exciting adventure to see God work in the lives of people who didn't know about the love of God and of Jesus."

"Did she tell you how hard it was going to be?" Debbie questioned.

"Will God help us now?" Cathy inquired.

Harold then spoke up with a gleam in his eye and an enlightened expression on his face. "Let me tell you a story. When I was a little boy, I didn't have any grandparents. They had all died before I was born. But an older couple down the road from our house treated me like their grandchild and I adopted them as my grandparents. I called them Papa Bob and Mama Ruth. Mama Ruth always kept warm homemade bread pudding in her warming oven just for me. I would go there everyday after school to visit and to get my bread pudding." Harold continued with a big smile radiating his excitement about being able to share his story. "In the living room of their home hanging over the fireplace was a big picture of a little boy and a little girl walking over a broken swinging bridge during a bad storm as the lightening flashed from black storm clouds. The children looked so afraid but standing tall behind them and in front of the storm clouds was an angel protecting them. This picture fascinated me and many times, Mama Ruth told me that an angel from God was protecting me too and she told me not to be afraid. So I suppose the Bible teacher, Mama Ruth, the picture, and a spark of adventure caused me to want to share the story of Jesus in a faraway place."

"Thanks for telling the story again. I'll try not to be afraid anymore." Cathy blurted out.

"Thanks for sharing Daddy. I love you." Janice interrupted.

I sat still wanting this moment to last forever.

September 28, 1964

Dear Mother and Daddy,

We finally got our 100 pound sack of flour. The newspaper reported that Ghana did not have any flour. We went to the government warehouse a couple of days before this was reported. A great crowd of people were standing, pushing, shoving and fighting outside the warehouse trying to buy flour. Armed with prayer, Harold was able to work his way inside of the warehouse and get the flour. Other food supplies still remain very scarce. Merchants in Kumasi told us that they do not expect any more shipments until December.

In April and May we made a special plea for prayers that God would send someone to Ghana to help us. God has answered that prayer in a most unusual way. Last Sunday we got a letter from a couple planning to come to Ghana. They told us that they were going to the Cameroons instead and would not be coming to Ghana. However, in the same mail we received a letter from Jim Kummel, a Peace Corps Volunteer, telling us that he had just arrived in Ghana. He is a Christian from Waco, Texas. He wanted information from us so that he could start attending church services with us. He is a school teacher and will be teaching in the beautiful science lab at the Sadler Baptist Secondary School that the Ghana Government just took over. We rushed over, greeted Jim and took him to worship service.

Jim is a very mature, warm, friendly twenty-one-year-old. He manages quite well considering that he is crippled. One leg is about 3 to 4 inches shorter and much smaller than the other. The children are very fond of Jim and he is a great blessing to us already.

Jim's Peace Corps appointment came in a very unusual way. When Jim graduated from college in May, the Peace Corps notice had not come in the mail. When he left his off campus apartment, he asked his neighbor to watch for the notice. One day she happened to see the yellow telegram in the door. She rushed to give it to Jim and he barely had time to keep the appointment. He did not choose to come to Ghana. The Peace Corps chose him to come to Kumasi out of the forty-two schools available. His mother was very skeptical about Jim coming to Ghana and doubted that the Lord was leading him there. Jim was very anxious to tell her how he was the answer to our prayers!

Harold and John are out preaching tonight at a mountain village called Nsuta which is a long distance from here. A man from Nsuta was recently baptized and wanted to start a church there. He is a preacher from one of the other churches. He took the Bible Correspondence Course and has many others interested in taking the course. This week a fifteen-year-old boy from Kononga took the Bible Course, then traveled 40 miles to be baptized. Harold and John just got home safely. They had a great campaign and many people came.

Thanks again for your help in the fund raising effort. The children are holding up like little troupers. Diana mentioned that Janice cries sometimes at night because she had practiced so much all summer long to be Snow White in the play at Ridge School. When the money ran out, we had to take the children out of Ridge School. She missed her big moment. Debbie spends a lot of her time in her room playing her violin. This seems to relieve a lot of her stress. Pray for the children.

Love,
Jane Ann

Early October 1964

While I was in the bedroom/office working on the monthly Ghana Report, I overheard Janice talking to John.

"John, why did you and Daddy stay out so late yesterday?" Janice questioned.

"We went to a village about an hour away with a man to see his sick mother." John replied.

"What was wrong?"

"She had leprosy."

"Did you see her?"

"Yes, when we arrived at the village, we went inside a small mud hut. She was lying on the floor on a mat. Her ears and toes were lying on the floor beside her. Whew! It smelled really bad!"

"What did you do next?"

"Daddy and the man picked her up and put her in the Microbus. Then we drove her to the hospital. It was a long drive. Daddy said it took us over two hours to get to the hospital."

"What causes leprosy?"

"Daddy said leprosy comes from not having clean clothes to wear and not taking a bath in clean water."

"Did Daddy say she didn't take a bath?"

"No, Daddy said they use dirty water to take a bath."

"Is our water clean?"

"Yes, Daddy said it is clean."

I heard the outside door open and close as their voices faded away.

October 7, 1964

Dear Mother and Daddy,

Harold has had three attacks of malaria last month. Dr. Bowesman was in U.K. on leave. Harold seems to be all right now.

We are getting ready for Janice's birthday party. We had to delay the party because of Harold's illness and dealing with other problems. Harold has been very depressed after the Bible Training School was forced to close. He is still waiting for a reply from the elders. He received a telegram from them last week saying: "Increased working fund probable. Your trip home is inadvisable. Pray."

We have not heard any word since. Yesterday we learned about new developments here. We cannot get any food or supplies into the country unless Harold leaves and brings it back as unaccompanied baggage. Then it will come in custom free.

All import licenses have been revoked. Prior to this, the government has not allowed any goods to come for several months. The goods sit on the dock for months while the people who imported the goods are charged fifteen dollars a day dock rental. Some goods have been on the dock six months. The Ghana Government confiscates all the goods if the dock rental is not paid. I thank God that we were able to get the 100 pounds of flour and sugar. Our steward goes to the market very early every day to buy vegetables and meat.

Jim Kimmel, the Peace Corps volunteer is such a blessing for us. He goes with us out in the bush nearly every Sunday for church services and then comes home with us to eat and visit. We plan to take three Peace Corps volunteers with us to Suminakese next Sunday and then have all of them over for dinner. They enjoy having parents away from home and we love having them. They are all just kids about 20 years old and just out of college. It is amazing how much enthusiasm they all generate.

Our good friends, the Bill Arnold Family, the Baptist missionaries, who just returned to the States on a one year leave, will not return. Bill has developed a serious heart condition. Six years ago he started the Sadler Secondary School and last May the Ghana Government forced him to give it to the Ghana Government. The Arnold's are lovely gracious people. Pray for them.

Love,
Jane Ann

October 13, 1964

Dear Mother and Daddy,

We went to Obuasi last Sunday. Obuasi is a gold mining town with a population of about 26,000, and boasts of having the largest gold mine in the world. The mine employs 6,000 people. This is the original mine and they go down 700 feet to get gold. It is a beautiful town and very clean. Most of the population is Muslim. (Adams 123-128)

The congregation in Obuasi was started 3 or 4 years ago and fell away. Recently one of the new preaching students started contacting

154

some of the brethren there. On Sunday we had a large attendance with five very influential men attending. One of the men, Brother Appiah, manages a fishing corporation. He recently built a new store building with living quarters attached. He announced that he had never been successful until he became a Christian. Now that God has blessed him so abundantly, he wants to give the church the store building for worship service and the living quarters for a preacher's home. The student preacher in Obuasi is a former Muslim. We are so pleased about the work. Pray for them.

A friend of ours at the bank is now working fulltime closing down banks in the bush. Ghana Commercial Bank will do all the banking now.

Debbie and I are making great strides in the school work! She made an excellent grade on her last arithmetic exam. She is an excellent seamstress. She made her first dress all by herself last week. She did a great job and it fits her perfectly.

Pray we can open up the Ghana Bible College soon. Harold is extremely anxious and depressed because he has not been able to find a place for the College to meet and of course, no money. Thanks for all your help with the fundraising.

Love,
Jane Ann

October 20, 1964

Dear Mother and Daddy,

We just received the letter you sent to us Air Mail nine days ago. The mail is really getting very slow.

Daddy, I am so sorry you have been sick! I'm sure that it is partly because of the extra burden you have taken on—the Ghana fundraising effort. Slow down and get proper rest. I am sure you will be blessed greatly for all the effort you have expended to expand the borders of the Kingdom of God. Paul certainly suffered for Christ. Many of his writings in the Scriptures tell how his sufferings were used to glorify God, and in that mindset he was able to find joy in his suffering.

Do not be concerned about me getting sick again like my ordeal in Santa Ana, California. It has been a thrill to me to know that God has been with me and blessed me richly. It is such a comforting, secure feeling to know that so many individuals and entire congregations are praying for us. We can see daily the providence of God. Alma Gatewood always said, "God's daily little miracles". Alma was assured that every little incidence, no matter how insignificant, was God's providence working on her behalf in her life.

We have sufficient amounts of food now. However, we must travel to Accra to purchase most of it. Yesterday we had tea with the mother of John's best friend, Pip Gudgeon. The mother is Cathy's teacher and the father is the President of Barclay's Bank. They had lived in Ghana over six years. They are leaving tomorrow for England and will be gone four to six weeks. Mrs. Gudgeon told us that the bank is transferring them to Accra after their vacation. The trend now is for Ghanaians to take over everything so fewer British people are here. She also said that Ridge School is suffering greatly now for lack of teachers.

We are taking Jim Kimmel and three other Peace Corps volunteers to the movie this evening. They are way out in the bush with no transportation to Kumasi.

One of the preachers, Samuel Young, the oldest preacher from Koforidua wrote saying that his wife gave birth to a son and named him Harold. It really thrilled Harold to know that. The second generation of preachers and preacher's wives will be Jerry, Harold, Jane (after Jane Davenport) and Jane Ann.

Love,
Jane Ann

This is a report that Debbie prepared as a school project.
October 20, 1964
Building a House in Ghana

Ghanaians are building a four-family house next door to our family's home in Kumasi, Ghana. Ghanaians build houses here much different than in America. Most of the workers are women who do the same work as men.

The first step to building a house is mixing cement. Women take big pans, fill them up with sand and carry the pan on their head to the cement mixer. Women carry everything on their head.

The next step is making cement in a cement block machine. The workers work steadily. The clanging of the blocks is heard from the noisy machine. They beat on the carrying pans as they sing. They work from six in the morning until six at night. They always laugh and sing while they are working.

Only the wealthy people can afford a cement block house. Poor people live in houses made of red mud. Some have a thatch roof, but the modern roof is tin because it will not leak.

This cement house will house four families with three rooms per family. The three rooms are bathroom, bedroom and family room. Poor families do not have a kitchen because they always cook and eat outside. They eat out of one common pot. They do not use eating utensils but eat with their hands. Most cement houses get painted. The finished house is then ready to use.

Deborah Kay Derr

October 30, 1964

Dear Mother and Daddy,

We received your letter and are very happy that Daddy is well again. We are at the end of the rainy season here. It is very cool now especially at night. Most everyone has a cold.

We received a letter from the elders at Cedars. They do not want Harold to go back to America alone. They want all of us to take a family vacation to Nigeria and then bring in food and supplies.

We plan to leave by boat on December 14 for Lagos, Nigeria and will arrive in Lagos the next day. We will take the VW Microbus with us and then drive to Ukpom and spend the Christmas Holidays with the brethren there. Eleven families and six young men will be there. We plan to return on the next boat January 19, or the following boat February 17.

The only way we can leave Ghana is by air or by sea—African Unity—we are very excited to be able to visit our friends in Nigeria. As you know, we had planned first to be working with them before Cedars approached us to go to Ghana.

We are really enjoying Jim Kimmel very much. He seems like one of the family now.

Love,
Jane Ann

November 4, 1964

Dear Mother and Daddy,

We heard the news this morning about the Johnson landslide. We do get some news from Voice of America Radio.

God has answered our prayers again and solved our problem about getting food and supplies. We are so excited about the elders at Cedars suggesting we take a vacation to Nigeria and they will provide the funds for our trip. In addition, they will arrange for us to bring in the needed food and supplies as unaccompanied baggage. The children are elated.

We see this entire scenario as the providence of God. Now we will be able to visit many of the dear saints that we had originally planned to work with: Doug Lawyer's, Rees Bryant's, Henry Farrar's, John Beckloff's and others. It will be so wonderful to enjoy Christian fellowship with our American brethren again and to enjoy singing hymns in English. Harold was asked to preach at a Government Secondary School last Sunday and conduct the worship service. Jim Kimmel led the singing. Afterwards in our home Bible class, John and Cathy both prayed very emotional prayers thanking God for sending us to a worship service where they could understand every word. The children will enjoy so much the missionary children in Nigeria.

The Lord does not seem to be leading us to reopen the Ghana Bible College until after we return from our vacation. We have been receiving many letters from young people saying that they saw the Ghana slides and now they want to devote their lives to mission work. Maybe the Lord's Will has been to inspire young people to be missionaries and not just send funds. So it seems that the Lord's Will has been accomplished, but not in the way we expected.

Jim Kimmel is now thinking about devoting his life as a high school level teacher for missionary children. Much good comes when large missionary groups can go together and work like in Nigeria.

Love,
Jane Ann

November 24, 1964

Dear Mother and Daddy,

Happy Thanksgiving! We have invited the Peace Corps Volunteers over for a Thanksgiving dinner. We have been collecting food for this for some time.

Life is becoming increasingly difficult here as Government controls tighten and the economy falters. All university students, most new Ghanaian Ambassadors and many senior civil servants must undergo indoctrination at the Kwame Nkrumah Ideological Institute.

Ghana's borders remain closed and there is much suspicion between Accra and the capitals of neighboring Togo, Upper Volta and the Ivory Coast. The bitterest anti-American campaign to date has started. The United States is no longer termed "neocolonialist" but "Fascist-imperialist". Even massive American aid is regarded as a scheme to make profits at Ghana's expense or to subvert the people.

While life here is uncomfortable for Westerners, it is becoming increasingly hard for Ghana's seven million people. Informed sources report that between 2,000 to 3,000 persons are being held under the Preventive Detention Act. All members of the 10,500 man Ghanaian army have become card-carrying members of the ruling Convention Peoples Party. Dues are deducted from their pay.

President Nkrumah dismissed Chief Justice Sir Arku Korsah earlier this year when the judge acquitted five high Government officials who had been charged with treason. The officials are now on trial again behind closed doors. President Nkrumah picked the judge this time and twelve young students from the Ideological Institute were chosen as jurors. Mr. Nkrumah has lately been appearing in public more often than in the month following an assassination attempt last January. He wears a bullet-proof vest under his Chinese military-style jacket. Some people now are taking the stand that anyone who associates with Americans are enemies of socialism. (New York Times 11/24/1964)

In spite of all of the political unrest, the Ghanaians are forging ahead with efforts to spread the Good News of Jesus Christ. The Kwaso church with eleven young boys and many children have saved their money, purchased land at the edge of town and have ambitious plans of planting cassava, selling it, saving the money and building a church building. Pray that their courageous devotion to the Lord may continue. A 30-year-old man traveled 165 miles just to be baptized. He completed the Bible Correspondence Courses. In other villages nineteen have been baptized so far this month.

Our little vacation trip has proved to be a lot of red tape. We cannot get the car out. All the borders are closed. The only way we can leave is to fly Ghana Air or Nigerian Air. It would take three pages to detail all the complications.

However, the providential hand of God allowed Harold to get a re-entry visa to Ghana for twelve months. Normally they make you fight for six months. This was essential in case we are forced out of Ghana. We would go to Nigeria first and stay with the brethren a few days before we go to the Cameroons.

Keep up the prayers. Everyday is a new challenge.

Love,
Jane Ann

December 4, 1964

Dear Mother and Daddy,
We had a lovely Thanksgiving American style with the Baptist missionary family. They served roasted chicken, dressings, sweet

potatoes, cranberry sauce, and pumpkin pie. They brought all of their food to Ghana with them. They have been here quite some time. They have two boys in Ridge School.

We have decided to take the children out of Ridge School the end of December because it is so expensive. Debbie is doing so well with the Calvert Correspondence Courses. It looks like I will be teaching all the children in January with Calvert material.

I have been extremely busy sewing for the children. I made about fifteen pair of panties and shorts and have ten more pair to make. I also have made several dresses for the girls. Our washing machine has been broken for three months. Yesterday, we finally got the needed part and were able to get it repaired.

We are going on a picnic tomorrow to Lake Bosumtwi and take four Peace Corps Workers. Many of the rocks around Lake Bosumtwi are known to have been placed there during the eruption of an ancient volcano. This sacred lake is 6 miles wide and very deep. It was caused by a tremendous volcanic explosion.

We asked John what he wanted for Christmas. He said he already has too much. He thought and thought and finally said he wanted an apple. He doesn't play with toys. He enjoys books very much but his favorite pastime is watching the Ghanaians build the house next door.

After the workers go home all of the children gather towels and native cloth together. They wrap cloths around them and play Ghanaian. Diana has watched the Ghanaian women so much that she can carry a baby doll or even John on her back, walk barefoot and carry baskets on her head. They all enjoy climbing up the mango tree in our yard. Cathy fell the other day but was only bruised—no broken bones. We go to the library every two weeks and everyone laughs at the huge stacks of books we carry home—usually eighteen. Then our house is very quiet until all the books have been read. Janice will read a book a day if we let her.

Harold is still working steadily on the model ship. He can't get a lot of the parts here so he is making them: propellers, wrench, anchors and furniture. Do you remember the model of the old sailing vessel he made for you before we were married? His high school yearbook even printed his picture standing by a model old sailing vessel that he had made. It had many beautiful sails.

Thank you for the Christmas check. The brethren in Terre Haute, Indiana, sent us a Christmas check for eighty dollars. They always send us a lovely Christmas gift every year. The Randolph's from Paris, Illinois, sent us a check for one hundred dollars as a personal check for us. They sent the sweetest letter that I will cherish for years.

Love,
Jane Ann

Early in December 1964
I wrote in my journal.

Early in December I wrote this entry in my journal. "Thank you God for helping me even when I made a terrible mistake! Cedars sent us a telegram on Saturday telling us that we could not draw out any more money from our bank account because it was overdrawn by one hundred dollars. I turned numb because I had no idea why this happened. To make the matter worse, we had no food and needed that money to buy food. On Sunday, we went out to the bush to one of the village churches. Harold used Psalms 23 as his sermon text. After worship services, we stopped by the Post Office. When we checked into our post office box to our great surprise, we found a letter from the Randolph's in Paris, Illinois. They had sent us a check for one hundred dollars to be used for the Derr family personally and not for the Ghana work. Later when I had time to check our bank statement, I discovered that the insurance draft for three months had not been deducted from our old American bank account that we had closed. The insurance company had just discovered this error and deducted all three months from our new account at one time! *Thank you God for covering my mistakes. Thank you, God, for loving me even when I fail miserably.*

December 9, 1964

Dear Mother and Daddy,

Last Saturday we took the Peace Corps Workers to Lake Bosumtwi for a picnic. The lake was made by a meteorite and is quite beautiful. Some people think the lake was caused by the eruption of an ancient volcano. The pagans who live around the lake believe it is sacred.

We parked as close as we could to the lake. Shortly, we discovered that the only way to get to the village by the lake was to walk about one and a half miles almost straight down a slippery, rocky, narrow mountain pass. Everyone went except me. I am no mountain climber. They were gone at least an hour or more.

I enjoyed talking to the people who walked by. The children are so loveable and friendly. They love to talk. Everyone wants a Bible or a Bible Correspondence Course. I watched a very elderly woman with a cane and a huge stone balanced on her head glide down the mountain path. She did not even watch her steps. She felt her way along with her cane. I wondered if she was blind. The boys told me that all the people who live around the lake can come and go only by way of this path and others like it. They walk this path every day. I felt weak and cowardly when I saw her.

Sunday we attended the funeral of a very devoted sister in Christ who died. She was only two years older than I. She died five days after her baby was born. She was in the hospital and requested prayer when some of the brethren were in her room. They all prayed. She finished the prayer, said amen and died. She lived in Suminakese. You would have been as proud as we were if you could have seen the funeral. It was truly a Christian funeral. It went against hundreds of years of traditional customs and pagan rites. Hundreds of people were at the funeral from many nearby villages and tried to bring in drums and pouring of libations. The brethren asked them to leave and continued in a Christian manner. This took great courage. It would bring tears to your eyes to see their faith and love.

We are planning to leave on our vacation December 21 and fly to Lagos, Nigeria. John Beckloff will pick us up and drive us to Ukpom.

Love,
Jane Ann

December 10, 1964

Yesterday was another unusually hot and muggy day, and today everyone is exhausted from our recent trip to Lake Bosumtwi and from putting together our plans for the trip to Nigeria. The girls are all quiet in their rooms reading the books that we got this morning at the library. Harold and John are out with some of the preachers running errands. So I decided now was a great opportunity to spend some time alone visiting with God.

I just couldn't get out of my mind the scenes I had witnessed at Lake Bosumtwi. I was relaxing under a large, shady tree on the bank of the river watching the swiftly flowing waters roll by. Suddenly the tranquility of this moment was abruptly interrupted by the sound of approaching footsteps.

As I glanced around I saw a little old Ghanaian woman emerge from the bush. She walked down to the edge of the river and picked up a huge stone. It must have weighed at least fifty pounds. I watched as she struggled to get it up into her arms, and finally onto her head. Then, carefully, she stepped down into the water. I watched as she waded farther and farther out into the river. The water reached up over her waist. But she kept going. Finally, she came up out of the water on the other shore, deposited her rock, and disappeared into the bush.

A great lesson was taught to me that day by this little old woman. She taught me that when we are weak, we become strong by increasing our burdens. She knew that the waters would sweep her down stream if she just waded in. She wasn't very large. But she knew by increasing her weight with the rock that her feet would be firm as she waded across the stream.

Then I read "And lest I should be exalted above measure by the abundance of the revelations, a thorn in the flesh was given to me, a messenger of Satan to buffet me, lest I be exalted above measure. Concerning this thing I pleaded with the Lord three times that it might depart from me. And He said to me, "My grace is sufficient for you, for My strength is made perfect in weakness." Therefore most gladly I will rather boast in my infirmities, that the power of Christ may rest upon me. Therefore I take pleasure in infirmities, in reproaches, in needs, in persecutions, in distresses, for Christ's sake. For when I am weak, then I am strong." (2 Cor. 12:7-10) Another Scripture said "I know how to be abased, and I know how to abound. Everywhere and in all things I have learned both to be full and to be hungry, both to abound and to suffer need. I can do all things through Christ who strengthens me."

(Phil. 4:12-13)

Here was a man who had found the secret of life: that in being made weak, he was made strong. He had found his strength in Christ Jesus. How was Paul made weak? By the infirmities in his flesh, by the distresses and the persecutions that he experienced, by the privations and by the imprisonments that he suffered. Paul was not, as he said, a sinner and because of that suffered these things. Paul was an Apostle of the Lord Jesus Christ and these were blessings—I call them blessings in disguise.

God, please strengthen me the same as you did Paul. I need Your help. I am so weak!

Wednesday December 30, 1964

Dear Mother and Daddy,

We were finally able to leave Ghana. We had everything all packed to leave Ghana on December 21. We drove to Accra and went to the airport. We were stunned to discover that Harold and I had both misread the ticket. Harold had asked for a night flight. The tickets were for a morning flight. So we were twelve hours late.

We left Kumasi on December 27 and drove to Accra to spend the night. The next day we flew to Lagos, Nigeria where we were met at the airport by John Beckloff. John had driven about 400 miles to meet us. We were saddened to learn that this was his second trip to meet us. He had not known that we had missed our first flight.

Early the next morning, we left Lagos and motored to Benin City for lunch. Hurrying on, we arrived at Onitcha just as the ferry was loading. Soon we were on our way across the Niger River. By nightfall we arrived at Onitcha Ngwa and were warmly welcomed by the missionary families there—Douglas Lawyer's, Rees Bryant's and Dr. Henry Farrar's. After eating the feast they had prepared for us, we all sang songs in the dark by the light of a small candle. The next day we drove to Ukpom where we spent much time enjoying the fellowship and hospitality of Don and Joyce Harrison, John and Dottie Beckloff, and Phil and Darlene Dunn. We enjoyed so much visiting each family.

We did not realize how much we missed Christian fellowship with American brethren until we arrived here. Our family is scattered. Some are staying with the Farrar's, some with the Dunn's and Harold and I are staying with Emily and Elvis Huffard's oldest daughter and her husband, Joyce and Don Harrison. They have been married only a year. Joyce and Don both teach at the new secondary school here. We plan to spend New Year's Eve with John and Dottie Beckloff.

One day we went shopping in the Aba market and were amazed at the availability of products. Aba is a fast growing city developing into a modern industrial city. The brethren in the two congregations in Aba have together purchased land on which to erect a new building. Our first impression of Nigeria and Aba was people everywhere and riding bicycles. Ghana has a population of seven million compared to fifty million in Nigeria. In Nigeria, the highways are narrow, coal tar roads. If you meet an oncoming car, your driver blows his horn and the two-wheelers scatter and head for the sandy shoulder. Your driver must do the same. This is done for safety reasons. Nigeria has many rivers and most of the bridges are one lane.

One memorable experience was taking a dugout canoe ride down the Qwa Ibo River at Ekot to the ocean. The Dunn's, Harrison's, Beckloff's, Bryant's, Rhode's, Marty Farrar, the Derr's, and six oarsmen all fit into three canoes. The canoes were hollowed out logs and if you were not balanced perfectly, the canoe would tip over. We carefully split all the families up. We carefully balanced the weights, realizing how important this was in preventing an accident. By splitting up all the families, an entire family would not be wiped out should there be an accident.

A Christian Secondary School has been built at Ukpom and is providing Nigerian boys and girls a secondary education with Bible emphasis. This year the school has been enlarged and shortly will be one of the finest secondary schools in the area. A new hospital adjacent to the Onicha Ngwa compound is being built. Dr. Henry Farrar is devoted to this work and spends many long hours of prayerful planning for this much needed Christian service. It was thrilling to stand on the campus at Onicha Ngwa and to think that this was once a great battleground in Nigeria's history. Today a Bible Training School stands on this ground where hundreds of young men have been trained to preach the gospel. This is testimony of the transforming power of the gospel of Christ.

It is so good to be here and to forget about Ghana for a little while. Harold wrote another article for the Christian Chronicle and you will probably see it in a few days. We are trying to raise funds for our return travel in case the Ghana Government asked us to leave on a 24 hour notice. Most all Americans in Ghana believe that we will be asked to leave by July 1965 when the Volta Dam is nearly completed. All Americans are living on a day by day basis. You are probably getting more Ghana facts than we are getting because all the news is controlled by the Ghana Government. They do not let any American Fascist Imperialists papers into Ghana. They are talking about closing down the American Information Service. We are kept well informed through the Peace Corps Workers and are assured that the US would take extreme action if they felt we were in immediate danger. We plan to go back to Ghana the last week of January. We will take many supplies back with us.

Love,
Jane Ann

This is a picture of the Derr Family in Nigeria just before we left for our dugout canoe ride.

This is a picture of our Nigerian dugout canoes. One memorable experience while we were in Nigeria, was taking a dugout canoe ride down the Qua Ibo River at Ekot to the Atlantic Ocean. The Dunn's, the Harrison's, Beckloff's, Bryant's, Rhode's, Marty Farrar and all

of the Derr Family along with six oarsmen carefully fit into three canoes. The canoes were hollowed out logs. If the passengers were not perfectly balanced, the canoe would tip over. We carefully split up all of the families and carefully balanced the weights. In case of an accident, we did not want an entire family to be wiped out.

Since I cannot swim and am petrified of water, I took in a deep breath and prayed that God would protect us. I could just imagine the canoe tipping over, and crocodiles rushing to devour us as we sank to the bottom of the river. I forced myself to focus on God's care for us, relax, and enjoy the moment.

PART THREE
1965

What do You want me to learn now, God?

"Those who sow in tears shall reap in joy. He who continually goes forth weeping, bearing seed for sowing, shall doubtless come again with rejoicing bringing his sheaves with him."
(Psalms 126: 5-6)

January 12, 1965

Dear Mother and Daddy,

It would be impossible to convey in words our thanksgiving to God for allowing us to be in Nigeria. We just got home from worship service at Ukpom. It is so refreshing and inspiring to be able to sing hymns in English, understand every word and to experience the warm fellowship of great saints. This will help us greatly to fill up our cup before we return to Ghana.

Harold is sick again. Dr. Farrar treated him for malaria five days ago. Now everyone here thinks he has dengue fever which is a very painful illness. Some of the symptoms are high fever, a rash, painful skin and depression. The treatment seems to be aspirin and time. He will go back to see Dr. Farrar tomorrow.

Our family is scattered. Diana is with the Farrar's 40 miles away. Cathy is staying with the Dunn's across the compound. We are staying with the Harrison's at Ukpom.

Today I taught my first ladies class at Ukpom. Joyce was sick and asked me to teach. About fifty women sat very attentively throughout the entire class and then they begged me to teach it again. I used flannel graph and had a great interpreter. The people here are very humble and beg to hear the gospel. It was a very humbling and joyful experience.

January 19, 1965

I couldn't finish the last letter because we've all been sick with malaria. Harold just got over what we think was sand fly fever. Malaria is more prevalent in Nigeria than in Ghana even though we sleep under mosquito nets here.

We read in Newsweek and Time Magazines that Ghana is planning an election in June and will change the currency from pounds to the decimal system. They stated that Ghana is a communist block African nation and is helping rebels in the Congo. We have not been able to get these magazines in Ghana. We continue to pray and we feel that the American government would protect us because over 2,000 Americans are here in addition to 150 Peace Corps Workers. We are trusting in God.

Love,
Jane Ann

February 1965

While we were in Nigeria, we discovered that the Ghana Government was reading all of our outgoing mail, so anytime we wanted to share problems that might be harmful to our safety, Harold would drive to the airport in Accra and give the mail to a passenger, requesting that the letter be mailed outside of Ghana. Harold took all mail written to Rees Bryant, a Nigerian missionary, to Accra airport to mail.

February 2, 1965

Dear Rees,

We arrived back in Nkrumah Land safely a week ago last Sunday. We had a very pleasant drive to Lagos. Patrick proved to be a very good driver. We appreciate so very much your fellowship, hospitality, and generosity in our behalf. It meant so much.

Our arrival here was not uneventful. We stepped into a new sales tax of ten percent. This means about twenty-one percent increase in the cost of living. The new sales tax, I believe, is the straw that will break the camel's back. The national budget was increased by one hundred percent. A large amount of this revenue will be supplied by this new sales tax. It is imposed at the wholesale level, and each time the merchandise changes hands the seller must add the ten percent sales tax, or sell at a loss of five percent on each item. Price controls are rigidly being enforced with very high penalties which will encourage consumers to purchase merchandise directly from the Government wholesale stores. This is causing many small stores to close and market women to stop selling. Foodstuffs are in very short supply. We were unable to find any bread yesterday. Kingsway and UTC stores have many bare shelves. Through the grace of God, we have two barrels of food at the harbor now going through customs.

The developments of January have convinced me that we should consider withdrawing from Ghana—at least until such a time when conditions here are more favorable. I have written a letter to the elders asking permission to leave about the last of March or the first of April. As I see it, in a short time there will be a duplication of the story you told me about the Ibo's and the Efik on your compound. Please convey this on to the elders at Cedars along with any other information which you feel the elders should know. We have asked permission to come to Nigeria, and stay a year before we return to the States, and then, Lord willing, to make a second tour of two years.

We plan to come on a visitor's visa and then to re-apply for a year's visa. Would it be necessary to deposit our return passage with the Nigerian Government in order to get the visa? We do not have any word as yet from the elders. We do not know if any money was collected from the article in the Christian Chronicle. We are in a quandary as to what steps we should take now. I am trying my best to continue to do all that I can here in Ghana. I am saddened to have to close down the Bible Correspondence School. The people here are so eager to learn.

Thank you for your prayers. I will keep you informed of the work here.

With Joy in His Service,
Harold

Early February 1965

My first goal after we got back to Ghana was to make sure the children continue with their studies since they have been out of school for so long. They are all avid readers so we went to the library and got many books about the people of Ghana.

Ghana History

The Akan in present day Ghana have linked their ancestry back to Medieval Ghana of the 4th to 13th Century. Geographically the old Ghana was 500 miles north of the present Ghana and occupied the area between the Senegal and Niger Rivers.

The Portuguese came in search of gold in the late 15th Century. They found gold in abundance adorning the powerful Ashanti kings of the Akan people. The Portuguese soon began construction of several forts along what came to be known as the Gold Coast. They began a written history of the area, plundered gold and shipped it back to Europe and got involved in the slave trade, which was their real money. The Portuguese traders fortunes attracted the Dutch, Danes and British in the late 16th Century. During the next 250 years, all four nations competed fiercely to control the trade, building forts and capturing those slaves of rivals. Nearly 10,000 slaves were traded annually. By the 19th Century 76 forts lined the coast—about one every four miles. Then slavery was outlawed in the 19th Century.

After the demise of slavery, the British took over the forts to use as customs ports, signing treaties with many of the local chiefs. The Ashanti profited handsomely from the arrangements, and their capital, Kumasi, began to take on all the trappings of a European city. The British grew increasingly uneasy with the tribes' wealth and influence, and when in 1873 the Ashanti refused to give up Kumasi, the British sacked the city and declared the Gold Coast a crown colony. Violent Ashanti resistance continued until 1900, when the tribe attacked the British fort at Kumasi, losing the battle but almost entirely destroying the city in the process.

The British set out to make the Gold Coast a showcase African nation, allowing few Europeans to settle or even be employed there. Cocoa exports became the backbone of the economy, followed by gold, timber, manganese, bauxite and diamonds. By World War One, the Gold Coast was the most prosperous colony in Africa, with the best schools and civil service, enlightened lawyers and a thriving press. Still anti-British sentiments ran deep.

In the late 1920's a number of political parties dedicated to regaining African independence began to emerge. In 1947, Kwame Nkrumah, the American-educated secretary general of the country's leading party, broke away from the group to form the Convention People's Party (CPP), aimed at the common person and pushing the slogan 'Self Government Now'. The CPP was an overnight sensation, and in 1949 Nkrumah brought the country to a halt by calling a national strike. The British responded by throwing him in prison, only to release him two years later after his party had won three general elections in his absence. Independence finally came in 1957, making Ghana—the name chosen by Nkrumah after the first great empire in West Africa—the first black African nation to win freedom from its colonizers. For Ghana, it was the beginning of almost 25 years of economic decline. Nkrumah borrowed heavily to finance the country. His most grandiose project, the Akosombo Dam on the Volta River, didn't bring the electrification and irrigation programs it promised for more than a decade. (Boateng Ghana History http://www.library.yale.edu) (Adamafio 7)

Musical Instruments

A national characteristic of the Ghanaian is their love of music. Song and dance are resorted to spontaneously in almost every phase of life at work and play; on the battlefield and at festive celebrations; at birth and on reaching puberty, and at death.

Some of the instruments they use are: clappers, gongs, pellet-bells, xylophones, jingles, and rattles; membranophones, all the variety of drums, wind instruments such as horns, pipes, flutes or stringed instruments including lutes, musical bows, harps and violins. The most commonly used are drums, flutes, horns, gongs and rattles.

Most of these instruments are used to provide music for the dance, but some are used for other purposes—providing rhythms for walking or working, giving signals or alarms, conveying messages, recounting the history of people, reciting proverbs and wise sayings or singing the praises of rulers or distinguished people.

The speech imitation of the talking drum is facilitated by the fact that the Akan language is tonal, or the meaning of a word may depend on the tone or pitch at which the syllables of a word are spoken and also the fact that the words are better understood in a sentence than when standing alone. (Kyerematen 57-66)

February 1965

One late afternoon, I observed the children talking and I quietly listened.

"John, do you like your life in Africa?" Janice inquired as she studied John's face for a response. "Is this what you expected?"

A line deepened between John's brow as he looked up in deep thought, "Well, no. Things are much different."

"What do you mean by that?" Janice continued to prod.

"I didn't see Tarzan or any monkeys. I like it here but it is a lot different."

"How is it different?"

"Well, there are lots and lots of beautiful lizards in my room." His face lit up and his eyes sparkled. "I really like those beautiful lizards. I want to pick them up." He frowned as he continued with, "Mommy won't let me."

"I sure don't blame her. Now what else is different?" Cathy interrupted.

"I like playing with the children here. I don't understand what they are saying. We just play games." John looked out the window. He face lit up as he blurted out, "Mommy wouldn't let me go barefoot like the other children. She said I would get worms. I got worms anyway!" His expression changed to a frown as he continued, "Mommy gave me that green stuff. Yuck!"

"Are you angry because you can't go to school?" Cathy asked with a puzzled look.

"Are you scared?" Janice questioned.

John came back with, "I like to go out in the bush with Daddy and the preachers. That's better than school."

"Aren't you scared going out in the bush?" Cathy quickly interrupted.

"What do you do, when you see the soldiers with guns, along all roads and all over town?" Janice inquired with a serious tone in her voice.

"I just take hold of Daddy's hand," replied John with great assurance in his voice.

As we sat around the table that evening finishing our meal, Cathy spoke up, "Daddy, I'm scared of the soldiers. I still dream about them every night."

Debbie jumped in with, "Daddy, last night I woke up and I was so scared. I was dreaming about soldiers coming in the house to hurt us," her voice softened as she continued with, "I saw them cutting off your legs."

Diana spoke up with, "I'm having scary dreams, too!"

"Daddy, what do you say to John when he is afraid? He goes out with you most of the time." Janice questioned.

Harold looked up quite unprepared to answer as he slowly scratched his head. He cleared his throat and replied, "Let's all hold hands and pray, and then I'll tell you a story."

After the prayers, Harold continued with, "One of my favorite stories in the Bible is in 2 Kings 6:14-17. This tells a story about Elisha, the prophet of God, who was surrounded by an army wanting to harm him. Let's read it, "Therefore he sent horses and chariots and a great army there, and they came by night and surrounded the city. And when the servant of the man of God arose early and went out, there was an army, surrounding the city with horses and chariots. And the servant said to him, "Alas, my master! What shall we do?" So he answered, "Do not fear, for those who are with us are more than those who are with them." And Elisha prayed, and said, "Lord, I pray, open his eyes that he may see." Then the Lord opened the eyes of the young man, and he saw. And behold, the mountain was full of horses and chariots of fire all around Elisha."

So children let's start looking for ways that God has helped us in the past and trust He will help us now."

As a thought crossed my mind, I spoke up, "Children, do you remember when we were living in the trailer at the Mill Creek Trailer Park? Daddy was out raising funds and we were very restless and anxious to leave and get on that plane headed for Ghana.

"Yes, Mommy, I remember how angry you were when you got that letter saying our visa had been delayed." Diana added.

"It was pretty bad," Debbie thoughtfully remembered as she spoke slowly.

"It was a sad day when we had to cancel our flight," Janice came back with.

"Yes, I remember," Cathy replied.

"I was stunned as Wendell read the newspaper article to me saying that our Swiss Air flight crashed in Zurich, Switzerland killing all 80 passengers on board. He said we were scheduled on that flight," Harold replied in a very serious tone of voice.

"Children, do you remember that our visa came in the mail the next day?" I related and continued with "Remember that God intervened and protected us and He will continue to protect us here now."

John excitedly spoke up with, "Daddy, tell the story about the mulberry bush."

Harold quickly smiled, opened up his Bible and surveyed the questioning eyes around the table. "Thank you, John," he answered and continued with, "The story that John is talking about is in 2 Samuel 5:22-24. This is a story about David. After David was anointed King, the Philistines went after David to battle. David went to the Valley of Rephaim and the Philistines followed. David asked God for help; God said he would defeat the Philistines. So David went to Baal Perazim and God defeated the Philistines there. However, when David went back to the Valley of Rephaim, the enemy followed David there. "Then the Philistines went up once again and deployed themselves in the Valley of Rephaim. Therefore David inquired of the Lord, and He said, "You shall not go up; circle around behind them, and come upon them in front of the mulberry trees. And it shall be, when you hear the sound of marching in the tops of the mulberry trees, and then you shall advance quickly. For then the Lord will go out before you to strike the camp of the Philistines."

Harold looked up at the questioning eyes and continued with, "We all need to pray every night before we go to sleep that God would open up our eyes to see His angels surrounding us with His love and protection. The first chapter of Hebrews tells us that angels are servants of God and are spirits sent to care for us. "Are they (angels) not all ministering spirits sent forth to minister for those who will inherit salvation?" (Hebrews 1:14)

So we need to look harder toward God and then He will remove our nightmares."

"Is God telling us, this is our time to wait?" questioned John.

"Yes, John it is." Harold quickly replied.

February 3, 1965

Dear Mother and Daddy,

Harold is out preaching in Obuasi about 40 miles away and the children are all in bed asleep. We had a lot of excitement immediately after Harold left. The children were all outside playing. Diana came running in to tell me that John had fallen from the top of the stairway inside the unfinished house next door. Debbie and Janice were carrying John toward me. He looked so pale and limp. The steward hailed a taxi for me and we rushed to the University Clinic near us. The kind doctor saw him immediately, examined him thoroughly and said, "Boys will be boys! He will be all right until he falls again."

The doctor was Ghanaian. He was so kind. He refused to take any money for his services. We were not even supposed to be there because the clinic was for University personnel. John scratched and bruised his back, knee, and head above the ear. He was so scared. That night in his prayers John thanked God for watching over him and taking care of him. When I inspected the place where John fell, I got a knot in my stomach. Many stones and cement blocks were strewn all around, but John fell down sitting in a sand pile. I think John has learned his lesson. He said he isn't going over there any more.

This past week, Evans Danquah, the preacher at Senfie, was notified that his uncle had died. According to Ashanti custom, Brother Danquah now becomes the head of the family. The family included the uncle's wives and children, other uncles and aunts, all nephews and nieces, Brother Danquah's own brothers and sisters and his own father and mother. Also according to their custom, the eldest brother of a woman is the head of her family, and not her husband. The family inheritance does not pass from father to son, but rather, from uncle to nephew. He is head over many persons who are actually his senior by many years.

Brother Danquah inherited the responsibility of providing for the uncle's wives and children in addition to a cocoa farm and all of the uncle's possessions. Included in the inheritance are all of the family gods and the altar. Each Akan family has its own particular gods. The main god contains the spirit of the family and is kept in a large brass container in the middle of the altar. It is to this god that the blood sacrifices are made. Also this god is fed with fufu, banana, tiger nuts, and peanuts. Many other idols are placed at the base of the altar. Some are for protection, prosperity, hunting, farming and longevity of life. The family gods are always kept in a special room in the house and only the head of the family has the key. Only the head of the family or the oldest woman, who must be past child-bearing, can enter this room.

Brother Danquah told us of his plans to destroy these family idols and altar which have been handed down for many generations. This requires a great deal of courage because the family is pagan and if they knew what he was planning, I am sure they would take very drastic measures. He said that he would secretly destroy these one by one. Although it will take several months to do this, he said by the grace of God he will succeed.

Some of the Ashanti customs are very strange to us. For instance, when a man dies, his wife or children do not inherit anything. This is because the wife was purchased and therefore is not a member of the family. However, the family may give her something if they believe she has been a good wife. Otherwise, they will turn her away.

After the husband dies, the wife is locked in her room for 40 days and is given palm nut soup once a day and fufu every 7 days. The American version of fufu—stiff mashed potatoes served with a hot pepper sauce.

At the end of the 40 day period she is prepared for a test to prove her faithfulness to her husband. First, a string of red peppers is tied around her neck along with the leaves of a plant that is very irritating to the skin. A plantain that looks like a large banana is then tied to her back. She is made to stand under a clump of leaves tied above her head. If she can jump and touch the leaves, this proves she is faithful. If she cannot, this proves she was unfaithful.

If she succeeds in touching the leaves, a clay pot filled with medicines is placed upon her head. She is then taken to the grave with the head of the family where she must weep and pray for her husband. At the end of the prayer, she stands and bends over forcing the clay pot to fall on the ground. If the pot breaks, it means that the spirit of the husband will not come back and bother her and the children. If it doesn't break, it means that he was not satisfied with her grief and prayers.

After this, she and the children must leave the house, and she is free to marry again. If she is too old to marry, then the person who succeeded her husband is responsible to provide for her and the children until they marry. (Rattray 171-174)

Now back on the home front, a new 10% sales tax has been imposed at the wholesale level, which means each time the merchandise changes hands the seller must charge the 10% sales tax. Price controls are rigidly being enforced with high penalties which will encourage consumers to purchase merchandise directly from the Government wholesale stores. This is causing many small stores to close and many market women to stop selling. Foodstuffs are in short supply. We thank God that we have two barrels of food at the harbor now going through customs. However, the local Ghanaians are suffering immensely.

The children are enjoying very much being home for their schooling. The Nigerian missionaries loaned us Calvert books until our books come in. Debbie is happier now that everyone is home. Some of their schooling is taking field trips into the villages to learn more about the Ghanaian people.

Love
Jane Ann

John watched an elderly man carve an Ashanti Stool from one solid piece of wood. Stool makers are highly skilled in their trade. Each Ashanti chief has his own stool. Each stool has a special story, and in times past, many were believed to have contained particular gods of the tribes. The carving began with a prayer or libation to the spirit of the tree out of which the wood is obtained, and to the tools being used—these might be knives, chisels or owls.(Rattray 272-273) (Kyerematen 76)

This is a picture of an Ashanti King Stool on the right. An Ashanti Queen Stool is on the left of the picture. Black stools were originally the special personal stools used by deceased rulers while alive. Upon their death, the ruler's stool was smoked or blackened by being smeared all over with soot mixed with the yolk of an egg. Then the stool is preserved in the memory of the ruler and is placed in the stool house. It is believed that the spirit of the ruler enters into or saturates his stool even while he is alive and this inhabitation persists after his death. The Ashanti people practice ancestor worship. Feeding of the ancestors is the underlying principle of the various national festivals. The pouring of libations is a belief that this will keep them in constant touch with their descendants, who will bless them through this act and if they do not do this, the ancestors will be angry and do them harm.(Meyerowitz Akan of Ghana 186-215)

This is Sasabonsam, or the bush devil, of the Ashanti Region of Ghana, West Africa. He is said to be a monster that lives in parts of the dense virgin forests. He has been described as being covered with long hair, having large blood-shot eyes, long legs, and feet pointing both ways. Many Ashanti people believe that Sasabonsam sits on the high branches of trees with his feet dangling down so he can hood the unsuspecting hunter. If any hunter goes into the forest and never comes out, the people claim that he was caught by Sasabonsam.(Rattray 27-28)

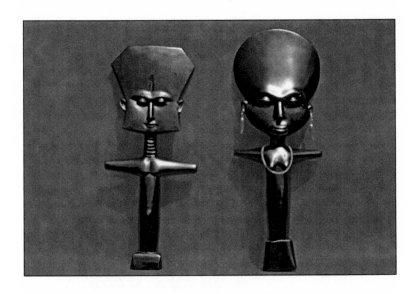

This is a picture of two Ashanti fertility dolls. Barren women will purchase one of these dolls. If she desires a male infant, she purchases the doll on the left. If she desires a female infant, she purchases the doll on the right. (Meyerowitz 130-131)

This is a picture of two fetish children. Since their mother was unable to bear children, she went to the fetish priest and he made

intercession in the mother's behalf to his god, with the under-
standing that when children were born, the mother was instructed
to not cut the child's hair until she had paid the full price of the
fee for the fetish priest's service. The mother of these girls had not
paid the fetish priest, so they could not cut the children's hair. This
is a common sight in the villages. (Rattray64-66)

The catfish is believed to be a representative of the bi-sexual sun
fertility god for one clan. There are only eight clans in Ashanti and
every lineage belongs to one or another of these clans. Every clan
is usually represented by a chief in every chiefdom. Each Ashanti
clan has an animal, fish, or bird that clansmen are forbidden to
kill or eat. The clan system is important as a unifying force in the
political organization and as an expression of the cultural unity of
the people (Meyerowitz, Akan of Ghana 48).

The catfish are fed by the priests at various places on the river Tano. We saw these catfish when a Ghanaian took us to this stream. We watched the catfish crawl onto the bank on dry land to be fed.

History records that the queen mother would plant a tree in the middle of the village in front of her house. A human sacrifice was then buried to ensure the well being of the village. The queen mother had to give her own daughter for this purpose. She could not rule until she made this sacrifice. To maintain life in the state, the queen mother was above all a rain-maker, and the annual festival centered on her power to produce rain for crops. In times of drought, women would go in procession to the sacred groves and pray for rain. (Meyerowitz Akan of Ghana 26-31).

Diana stood by the village refuge stone. It was the custom that a man who had committed a crime against the state could take sanctuary at the stone, or cone, under the place that marked the grave of the queen mother's sacrificed child. This was supposed to buy his favorable outcome for the trial. Such offenders were required to obtain an animal for sacrifice—a sheep or sometimes a fowl—and then they were taken away to be judged. Barren women could come and kneel before the figure and pray for children.(Meyerowitz Akan of Ghana 26-31).

February 10, 1965

Dear Grandma and Grandpa,

I hit the jackpot on mail today. I got a letter from you and one from Marty Farrar in Nigeria. Did I tell you about Marty's brother getting stung by a stingray? It was so painful that he cried for three straight hours without stopping.

Since we are not in Ridge School now, we read library books over and over again. Sometimes we sun bathe and spray each other with the hose. I made several games for us: a Clue Game; a Password Game and American Travel Game. We brought a Canasta Game from America so we play that sometimes. Tonight Debbie,

Daddy, Mother and I played Canasta. Mother asked me to play her hand while she made us popcorn. While she was gone, I played and Mother and I won.

Today we worked in the Bible Correspondence School grading papers, addressing envelopes and mailing them. The drums are really beating tonight. I think someone died. Daddy told us to write to missionaries in different countries to add to our collection of stamps. I have stamps from Ghana, India, England, Jordan, South Africa, Cameroons, Nigeria, Germany, China, Berlin, Spain, New Zealand, Canada, Australia and America.

Love Always,
Diana Lynn

February 11, 1965

Dear Harold,

I received your letter while I was in New York. I always think of the difficulties which Paul had and there are few places in the world today where the going is easy. You can be assured that as long as you are there, we will do our best to stand by you. Our trouble is knowing just what is needed.

Harold, keep me fully informed of your plans. God bless you. My prayers are ever with you. Use me while I live,

Love,
Jimmy Lovell

This was written as a school project.
February 12, 1965
My Life in a Foreign Country

My family and I are missionaries in Kumasi, Ghana, which is in West Africa. My life in Ghana is very different from life in America. Although we live in a cement house, Africans around us live in mud houses. Lovely wild flowers are all around the house. Tall, narrow trees which produce a fruit called paw paw grow wild in our front yard. Much fruit is grown in Ghana.

We buy our food from an outdoor market. Many market sellers sell many different items. Every market day the market sellers carry their goods on their heads. They all go very early to market so they can be ready when the first buyer comes.

Every Sunday my Daddy goes out into the jungle with some other African preachers. When the village people hear Daddy stop our car, they all start running to him. Daddy follows his translator and African preachers to the mud church building. After services Daddy gives medicine to the sick and bandages wounds. As Daddy leaves they all tell us bye. The only English word most of them know is bye. They also use this word as a greeting.

We do not have television in our home although Nigeria does. However, we have a very good radio instead. It is almost as good as a television. We are able to get "The Voice of America" very well.

I have a hobby that sometimes keeps me very busy. I collect stamps from many countries. A comic strip called "Garth" is printed every day in the Ghana newspaper called "Daily Graphic". A part of the story is printed each day. I enjoy reading it very much.

My grandparents sent us our boxer dog, Ginger. They sent her by air and she got here in real good condition. However, a month or two later, Ginger was killed by a lorrie passing by on the road in front of our house. We had another dog, Nutmeg and the same thing happened to her. Next we got two grey parrots. One by one they died. We have stopped having pets. Can you guess why?

These are just a few things that happen here in Ghana. We are all well and happy and live day by day.

Debbie Kay Derr

March 5, 1965

Dear Mother and Daddy,

We still have not heard from the elders at Cedars. The Nigerian quota has been raised from 11 to 33 now. We hope that we can go to Nigeria very soon, if not we will be back in the States as soon as the travel funds can be raised. The Nigerian vacation just made us more uneasy about the environment in Ghana. We have just committed the whole matter to the Lord and we know that He will settle it according to His will.

We went to Accra to buy food this week. The shelves in Kumasi have never been so bare. In Accra, we did get a good supply of most everything we need for a month. Then today, we got the barrel that we shipped from Nigeria. It contained three cases of communion wine and the rest of the space was filled up with food: pork and beans, dried beans, yeast, canned meat and tuna, cheese and oats. So we are all right now for food for a while. I feel that we will be in a much better mood now. It is quite depressing having to go to town everyday to hunt enough food for that day and then not find what you wanted. We just got the best pan of green beans out of our garden yesterday which was the first batch of the season. We had the best dinner today: pinto beans, ham and greens. We brought some yeast and raisins in the barrels so we are having cinnamon rolls tonight.

We just found out tonight that the Ghana Government has just stopped compulsory religious education in all of the schools and the University of Legon has closed down the religious department there. It is the University of Ghana at Legon. This looks like it is the beginning of the end of squeezing out religion in Ghana. The two largest chains of retail stores Kingsway and UTC have been taken over by the government store GNTC and Kingsway and UTC will leave Ghana the end of March. The Lebanese, Indians and Syrians are also leaving the end of March.

We are very busy packing. As Debbie is always saying, "We are all well and living day by day." We just had to fire the steward. We discovered that he has been stealing a lot of food.

Love,
Jane Ann

Early March 1965
I wrote in my journal

"After we got back from Nigeria, we found out that Ghana Government Officials were reading all of our outgoing and incoming mail. Because of Harold's prior nine year service with the United States Government, he was very cautious and never went to the American Embassy and tried to be extremely careful of his every action. So he always took any sensitive mail to Accra and gave the letters to passengers who were going to Nigeria and requested that they mail the letters. *God please continue to protect us!"*

March 5, 1965

Dear Rees,

I have a friend who is flying to Lagos this week so I thought that I would take this opportunity to give you some of the recent developments here. Things continue along the same Nkrumah lines. He has just finished a 14 day fast and there has been great speculation about where he was during this time. One thing is evident. The papers and radio are becoming extremely militant after he finished his fast.

The food situation has now reached its most critical stage. There is not sufficient stock in Kumasi to meet the needs. This past week we had to drive to Accra to buy food. We bought supplies for several other families also. The rumor is, and it is very strong, that all of UTC is pulling out of Ghana. They have already closed all of their stores in the north. From all indications they are making preparations to do the same thing in Kumasi. It looks as if Kingsway is also doing the same thing. Even in Accra, the only stores with ample supplies are the Government owned stores. The Government does not have a store here except to handle flour, sugar, and rice. They have no canned goods. Even the local food is getting very scarce and is the same price as imported. Along with the critical food shortage, we are beginning to experience strong anti-white feelings. Monday we went to 15 stores and 13 of 15 refused to sell to us. I think there are two reasons. First, the Ghanaian merchant is saving the products for Ghanaians, and the other reason, I feel, is that they are afraid for political reasons to sell to the white man.

I have been talking to some Lebanese and Indian merchants and they all said that in just a few weeks, there is going to be a mass exodus from Ghana. As you know, the Government will not let them take their money out or their possessions. It is my personal feeling that what they can't take out, they plan to burn. At the present time the Lebanese are offering fifty percent to anyone who will take their Ghana pounds and write them an outside check. Some of the Indians are offering seventy-five percent. We discovered in Nigeria that the Ghana pound is only worth ten shillings. In November the Ghanaian Times ran a series of articles about why the Lebanese, Syrian, and Indians had to be put out of business. It is no secret that the Government is doing exactly that and does not plan to issue any more import license until they leave.

Another recent event that has caused us great concern was an incident that happened about January to the Assembly of God missionary in Kumasi. A few weeks ago, he was stopped in Kumasi by a policeman. The policeman told the missionary his name, name of his wife and children, date they had entered Ghana, where he had been the previous Sunday, and many other interesting things. He also said that all American missionaries were under constant surveillance. They knew where we go and everyone who comes to visit us. Another important statement he made, "Why don't you Americans go home? The Congo is coming to Ghana and you Americans are going to get what you deserve!" The incident was reported to the American Embassy. The Assistant Chief of Police at Tamale, who is a member of the Assembly of God Church, when told of the incident confirmed that they had been instructed to keep surveillance on all Americans.

We were warned last week through the Peace Corps that there is a critical shortage of chlorine. So therefore, we must boil all of our drinking water now. We still have not received the barrels. We keep hoping everyday! We just received the barrel from Nigeria, but not from America.

We just received your letter with the customs regulation sheet and appreciate all of your efforts. We have sent in the Nigerian visa application. I would appreciate any help that you might give us in a letter to the elders at Cedars. It has been over a month since I have heard anything from them and so I do not really know what they are contemplating. In a prior letter, they had asked us to return to the States in June or July. We would like to spend one more year in the field, but we feel we cannot stay that long in Ghana.

Enclosed are some Bible Correspondence School enrollment forms for the Cameroons, Nigeria, and Ghana.

Your brother,
Harold

March 18, 1965

Dear Rees,

I am sending a short note to give you some more names for the Bible Correspondence Courses. An interesting recent development may have an important bearing on Bible Correspondence Courses in Ghana. The University of Ghana at Legon has closed down the Bible Department. It is strongly rumored that the government is taking Bible study out of the schools in April or September. The government will never make any official statement but a Baptist woman who teaches Bible in one of the large secondary schools has stated that it seems evident that the government intends to carry out this plan. This will either create a greater hunger for the Bible or will diminish it. The government is crowding ten years of education into eight, which means that the study load of the student is very heavy. Under the circumstances, the student will have little free time for the Bible studies.

The government has plans to unite the existing religious groups and form one national church. A committee was established in 1958 to work toward this goal. One of the preachers told me recently that a government official told him that the government is trying to stop many of the religious groups here. The food situation here is the same as I expressed in my last letter.

We still have not heard anything from the elders at Cedars concerning our future plans and the work here. Shortly after we returned to Ghana, I received a letter from them saying that I should close down the Bible Correspondence Office and curtail preachers support and all preaching expenses. They allotted me enough money to meet the house and utilities expenses and a little bit for gasoline. They are taking all the money to put in the return travel fund. Now I feel that I am accomplishing nothing. I have a study in our home with two French men from Togo and with a little preaching on Sunday that is about it.

Thank you very much for everything. We send our love to everyone.

Your brother,
Harold

March 22, 1965

Dear Mother and Daddy,

This letter will be very short. We are very busy. The elders wrote saying that they want us to go back to the States in May before the airlines increase prices for the summer travel season.

Harold is very busy studying with two young men from Togo. One young man is very well educated and speaks fluently French, German, English as well as his native tongue in Togo. He is very interested in the church and wants to preach the gospel and become a missionary. He is a very talented artist and has traveled all over West Africa. He now wants to go to the Bible Training School in Nigeria. The other man speaks French only and so this study is slow however we hope it is rewarding. Pray that they both may obey the gospel! We have written the missionaries in France for some French tracts and Bible lessons. The men come three times a week to study.

We had a lovely day Saturday. The Assembly of God missionary family in Kumasi invited us over for dinner. They brought 25 barrels of food with them and really prepared a feast for us. It was an old fashioned American Thanksgiving dinner: Baked turkey, dressing that melted in your mouth, gravy, canned corn with red pepper, lime punch, homemade ice cream and chocolate cake. Yum! Yum! We have not had any chocolate in Ghana for several months. Yes, cocoa is Ghana's biggest crop! We don't ask questions. We just accept it.

We went to Suminakese yesterday to church. They are really a wonderful group of people and the church is growing all the time. The preacher there supports himself as a tailor and is doing a great job. After every service all the members go together to the homes of all of the sick members and sing hymns and pray for them.

Debbie and Diana are studying French three times a week with the Peace Corps couple across the street. They are both French teachers.

Love,
Jane Ann

April 4, 1965

Dear Mother and Daddy,

We have had some company from America and Nigeria. Everett Anderson, who is raising funds for the Nigerian Christian Schools Foundation, came to Accra. John Beckloff, from Nigeria, came with him. We were so glad to see them! They had planned to just be here a few hours but their plane broke down in Lome, Togo and completely tore up their plans. They are flying to Sierra Leone to take care of some important business. A man has given the church a large school and they are trying to get missionaries to go to Sierra Leone. They were forced to be in Ghana four days! John Beckloff flew to Kumasi to visit with us a couple of days. Everett Anderson had to stay in Accra to make sure the plane reservations were correct. They said they felt the Lord wanted them to stay in Ghana a while and we sure were glad and thanked God.

I will write again soon.

Love,
Jane Ann

April 7, 1965

Dear Rees,

Greetings from Ghana! We just had an enjoyable visit with John Beckloff and Everett Anderson. We were so thrilled that they were able to spend some time in Ghana. They were taken off of their plane to Togo because of mechanical difficulties, and were unable to keep their plane schedule. Because of this, they were able to stay in Ghana for four days. We enjoyed their fellowship very much and their impressions of Ghana.

I have been studying privately with two young men from Togo three nights a week. They are both very much interested in New Testament Christianity and are both very able students. One young man speaks German, French, English and his own native tongue. He is well educated and maintains himself as an artist. He came wanting to attend the Ghana Bible College, and has said that he wants to preach. We are praying that this is possible. I have written Brother Wright in France for some French literature and Bible Correspondence Courses to be distributed in Lome. The Baptists started a mission work in Togo about a year ago. They are very pleased with the results. The Assemblies of God have 15 families in Togo and report that it is a more fruitful work than Ghana. They both send their missionaries to France for one year and then to Togo.

Attached is another list of Bible Correspondence applications of eager students and another list of men who want to attend your Bible Training School.

Things here continue to be very explosive. John Beckloff can give you a full report. John mentioned having some of the Nigerian brethren spend some time in Ghana this summer preaching and encouraging the brethren here. We pray this can be arranged as this would do so much to encourage and strengthen the bonds of love between them.

We have just received a letter from the elders at Cedars suggesting that we return to the States before May 20th as the plane fares increase after that date. This would give our children an opportunity to enroll in summer school. We plan to spend about two weeks in Wilmington and then Jane Ann and the children will spend the summer in Terre

Haute, Indiana with my parents while the children are in school and I will go to California. We hope to locate somewhere in the Los Angeles area so that I can attend classes at Pepperdine.

Our prayers are with you in the good work that you are doing. Love and best wishes to all.

Your brother
Harold

Harold and Jane Ann wore their Kente cloth garments to church worship services. Ghana is famous for its weavers of Kente cloth. It is woven in narrow strips about four inches wide. Four different weave

patterns can be distinguished in a strip, which together give the cloth a checkered design. Now all the designs are given names. Most of the designs can be worn by anyone, however, the design called the consumer of fire is a restricted design for the Asantehene on his accession to the Golden Stool, and at death is spread on his corpse when lying in state. In the past, it was the custom for all designs to be shown to the King of Ashanti. Those designs which he particularly liked, he reserved for his exclusive use; others he allocated to the princes and princesses, and to other great men and women in the Kingdom.

As in the case of the King, these designs were then worn only by the men and women to whom they had been allocated. Just as the Scottish clans have their tartans, so families and clans of the Gold Coast (Ghana) had their kente of exclusive design.

The clan, or social status, or sex of the weaver was represented by a pattern which had its own name. For example, the design, "Adveneasa" which translated means, "my ideas have come to an end." That is, I have put all of my ideas into this design and all my skill into this kente.

The art of weaving in Ghana was first practiced by the peoples of the north and is said to have been introduced in the seventeenth century by Otaa Kraban, an Ashanti from Bonwire, the village best known in Ghana for the making of kente cloth. In the beginning, these cloths were woven in white and navy blue cotton threads which were grown, spun and dyed locally. When the Dutch came, they introduced silk cloth. The weavers then patiently unraveled the bright colored silk threads and incorporated them into the kente cloth. Before this, weavers used the yellow thread spun by large black and yellow spiders. In the same way, the silk worm's thread was used in the weaving of silk cloth.(Kyerematen, Akan of Ghana 74-78)

Sunday April 11, 1965

Dear Mother and Daddy,

We went to church this morning at Obuasi. It was the last time we were able to go there. Everyone told us good-bye. They were all so sweet and it was so difficult to think we can't go back to see them. Sister Appiah gave Cathy her gold necklace and they gave us pineapple, bananas and oranges. We went to Brother Appiah's and had refreshments. We left home this morning at 8 and got home this afternoon at 2. We weren't able to eat lunch until 3. We had company Sunday morning and didn't get to eat breakfast so we were starved by then. We have had four batches of company today and the two men from Togo are coming tonight for Bible study and it looks like they will both be baptized, opening up the gospel into Togo—French speaking Africa.

We received a letter from the elders at Cedars recently. They want us to return to America before May 20th because the airline rates go up after that and then we can enroll the children in summer school in Terre Haute. We are planning to go to Accra in the morning to reserve space on the plane. I think it will be probably be May 18th.

We are busy getting things rounded up and barrels packed. It is a lot of work sending them out now as the forwarding agency does not have a branch in Kumasi—only Takoradi. The one in Kumasi closed last June. We still do not have the barrel that Wilmington sent to us. We did locate it and hope to pick it up ourselves in Accra. It has been only four months that we have been trying to get this barrel.

I will write again soon.

Love,
Jane Ann

April 11, 1965

Dear Grandma and Grandpa,

How are you? I am fine. On Sunday we went to Obuasi. Daddy told the members that we were not going to go to Obuasi again. Mr. Appiah invited us to go to his house. Mrs. Appiah was so sorry that we were leaving that she gave me a gold necklace. The other girls said they would buy a necklace. I got my hair cut down town by a girl named Janet. While Daddy and John were waiting they went to the library. They have nice books. Tonight we are going to the Cinema. We go there nearly every week because we don't have a television.

Good-bye for now.

Love,
Cathy

Late April 1965

After spending several hours packing the barrels that we were shipping back to the States, I took a deep breath and decided to take a short break. My eyes stopped at the sight of a red, leather bound journal as I scanned the huge pile of items yet to be packed. I picked up the journal out of curiosity to see the date. Thumbing through the pages, an entry marked May 25, 1963 caught my attention and I read, "We ate a delicious, big breakfast, cleaned the trailer and by 9 A.M. we were on our way to see the Grand Canyon. We visited the village, the Exhibit House and then went to the museum. After viewing the canyon through binoculars, we heard the lecture about the Grand Canyon story. 'The Grand Canyon did not come into existence all at one time. There was no cataclysmic earthquake to form this great chasm. It was the slow, steady cutting away of the Colorado River into the gradually rising crust of the earth that gave us this gorge—one mile deep and averaging about ten miles from rim to rim. Persistent wearing away of the land by summer rains and winter snows helped to give width to this tremendous canyon.'

As we stood gazing into the canyon, trying to force ourselves to comprehend the processes that created it, we were aware of the silence and the lack of any movement against this giant-sized backdrop. We just noticed a few clouds passing by in the distance. My heart was overwhelmed with awe viewing God's great masterpiece. How vast is eternity and how short a human lifetime.

Is God presenting me a lesson today? Is He telling me that he wants me to have persistent, slow but steady spiritual growth? Is He telling me that it is not some great deed like an earthquake that gets God's work done, but it is persistently doing my Christian duty, not shaken by the adjustments life demands of me—sorrow, pain, sickness, disappointments and other life shaking events? Is God telling me that such a life will have a tremendous impact? Is He saying that a life of slow, steady spiritual growth by praying, studying the Bible, meditating, and obeying God's commandments daily is what He wants?"

I put the journal down and my thoughts turned to our devotion today at the dinner table. Harold had been trying to prepare the children for all the adjustments that they are going to need to make as we prepare for our new life in the States. He always tries to capture their attention with a funny story with an impact. Today, Harold told a frog story.

"Children, I am going to tell you a frog story today." Harold began.

"Daddy, are you going to tell about the times you got up in the middle of the night and tried to kill the frogs making all that noise in the baptistery?" Diana blurted out.

"Remember how John Law heard you and got his machete? He killed the frogs!" Debbie chuckled.

"No, this is a story that a scientist told me." Harold replied and continued with the story.

"A scientist placed a lively frog into a container of water. He then heated the water very, very slowly at the rate of about three percent of a degree every minute. The frog enjoyed his new environment very much. As the water got hotter and hotter, the frog just seemed to enjoy it all the more. He thought it was so much fun. Finally, when the temperature of the water had reached 140 degrees, the frog died. From all observation, the frog experienced no discomfort. The frog did not try to escape. It appeared that the frog enjoyed the experience until the end.

Sin or disobeying God's instructions are somewhat like the frog and the water. Since sin is so slow to affect us, and we are so slow to react, suddenly, without warning, sin overtakes us, and destroys us, and we are not even aware of what is taking place."

Harold's last words penetrated my soul, "The weak give up and the strong almost do."

May 10, 1965

Dear Mother and Daddy,

Harold left over two hours ago to direct a truck to our house to pick up our barrels and still no sign of him. John Law has hired some workers to help load the truck and now a rainstorm has come. We have been trying somehow to get the barrels to the pier for quite a long time and it seems something always hinders it.

We are planning to go to Accra tomorrow to take care of the tickets. We shudder to think about what complications will arise there. We must pay a new 10% sales tax on our plane fare raising the cost of the tickets $300.00.

We plan to be in Wilmington from May 21 to about June 4th. You can send our mail to Cedars and after that to Terre Haute.

May 11, 1965

I was not able to finish the letter yesterday. Many surprising events happened to hinder this. First, after 2 ½ hours I decided to take a taxi to find out what happened to Harold. Just as I started to leave, he came driving in. On the way to town the clutch cable broke on the VW and by the grace of God, Harold got it to the repair shop. They had the part and after much palaver decided to fix it then. Afterward Harold went to Tarzan, the forwarding company, and they could not take our things because their truck was broken down and had to be repaired first. So this morning Harold is at Tarzan again trying to get these things moved today. Our Accra trip will need to be postponed until Thursday. This is a typical day in Africa. It takes all week to accomplish all the tasks you started out to do on Monday.

Another day has gone by and I haven't been able to finish this letter. We did finally get our barrels to Tema ready to go to America. We just got back from Accra today. We left at 4 A.M. and got home about 6 P.M. I have our tickets to America in my purse and our barrels are at the dock in Tema. The only thing we must do now is to wait one more week to leave.

I will write more when I have time.

Love,
Jane Ann

Late in May 1965

Our last week in Ghana was very emotional. It tore at our hearts witnessing the contrast of the Ghanaian's craving for every crumb of God's Word, and then experiencing the indifference of the American brethren to support us. Tears came to my eyes remembering how many poor widows gave to help each month, and the prosperous people ignored our letters and pleas for financial assistance. I thought about Jimmy Lovell and his "Miss a Meal Program" and how willing he was to help us—he was a rare jewel. Our emotions were worn down by all the farewell parties and gifts.

All too soon, we were on the airplane headed for America. I smiled when I thought about the surprised and proud expressions on the faces of the Ghanaians when they saw me wear my new kente garment on our trip home to America. From my seat on the plane, I glanced over at the children and could see the big smiles on their faces as they excitedly talked about seeing their grandparents again, going out for a hamburger and fries, being able to go to the World's Fair in New York. Then I looked over and saw Harold's downcast expression. I wondered if he was thinking the same thing that was running though my mind? How would he find a new job? It takes a long time to find a church needing a preacher and we did not even have time to develop his new resume. Where would we live? We had no car. The only home we had was a 17 foot trailer that we were still making payments on. Where would the money come from? We had exhausted our savings. How about the children? I was so concerned that they have had no formal schooling in nearly a year. Will they be able to keep up with other American children their same age? I felt lost and disconnected and so unsettled about our future.

I reached over and squeezed Harold's hand. He leaned over and whispered in my ear, "You will always be my beautiful bride." I was thankful for his attempt to reassure me. Over the next several hours I reflected about our life in Ghana and how God had taken care of us there. Our needs were so great, and I prayed that He would continue to care for us now with our many concerns. I was coming to the realization that while my faith had been greatly tested in Ghana, embarking on this new journey will take a deeper act of faith. It would be like walking on the water.

Before I knew it, the pilot was announcing our initial descent into New York. As we flew through the clouds, we started to circle, waiting for our approach to land. Suddenly, I caught a glimpse of the long awaited sight of the Statue of Liberty. I was overwhelmed with relief when I saw this flame of freedom. It reminded me of the strong contrast of the country we left in fear, and now we would be home surrounded in freedom.

When we arrived at New York International Airport, the medical officer in charge of the U.S. Quarantine Station detained us. A passenger on our flight had smallpox so we were ordered to be revaccinated for smallpox and yellow fever. Next we were placed in quarantine until June 4 in Wilmington, Delaware. They allowed us to stay in the home of Ernie and Katie Hynes, under the supervision of the U.S. Quarantine Office. We had to call the Quarantine Officer assigned to our case every day to report the status of our health. To our delight no one got sick.

To add to our concerns, several officials at the airport told us how fortunate we were to be able to flee the country safely. Americans who had arrived at New York International Airport from Ghana on the previous day had been imprisoned for several weeks in Ghana for conspiracy and espionage.

While we were in Wilmington, Delaware, we had the opportunity to visit with many wonderful saints at the Cedars Church of Christ. They shared their homes, wonderful meals, listened to our stories and made sure that we were able to acquire a dependable station wagon. The children were very excited about being turned loose in the church benevolent room. John called this room "the overseas store". We all collected many treasures to wear on our next journey with God.

We are all snowflakes and everyone is unique. God uses flawed, willing people and has a special purpose for each person. This was His special purpose for us.

What is God's purpose for you?

PART FOUR
2007

Epilogue

"Behold how good and how pleasant it is for brethren to dwell
together in unity."
(Psalms 133:1)

It has been a thrilling experience for me to discover the exciting
current mission efforts in Ghana as God enabled me to connect
with so many people who willingly shared their stories. It is so
inspiring to witness first hand what wonderful things can happen
when brethren work together sharing their many diversified talents
all for the one goal of sharing the magnificent story of Jesus, the
Christ and the goodness of God, the Father.

"My little children, let us not love in word or in tongue, but in deed
and in truth."
(1 John 3:18)

"No one has seen God at any time. If we love one another, God
abides in us, and His love has been perfected in us. By this we
know that we abide in Him, and He in us, because He has given us
of His Spirit."
(1 John 4:12-13)

HISTORICAL REVIEW OF GHANA MISSION WORK
1961 TO 2007

"By God's power and grace the church continues to grow in Ghana. Today's success in Ghana is the cumulative effort of many workers. At least a hundred individuals and families have lived in Ghana and done various mission works. The key to success has been the involvement of Ghana Christians in the work. Every key work in Ghana is in the hands of the local Christians. They teach, preach, print, do health care work, teach health care, operate the schools, send out missionaries and support them, plan and evangelize, often with much greater success than the American workers." reports Jerry O. Reynolds.

The mission work in Ghana, West Africa began in 1961. The family of Jerry Reynolds and Dewayne and Jane Davenport were the first missionaries from the Church of Christ in Ghana. An American Christian sent Bible Correspondence Lessons to John Gaidoo in Accra. Nigerian missionaries followed up on this contact and John Gaidoo was baptized. After learning of this, Jerry and Dewayne planned in 1961 to move to Accra and work with John Gaidoo.

When they arrived in Accra, August 1961, soon they discovered that John Gaidoo had died a month earlier. The next discovery was that Accra, the political center of Ghana, was in great turmoil. Kwame Nkrumah, the president had declared Accra and the area around, under martial law. He had imposed a 6PM to 6AM curfew, which would greatly hamper nightly preaching. After prayer and study, Jerry and Dewayne decided to investigate Kumasi, a large centrally located city in the Ashanti Region of Ghana. In Kumasi, they found adequate housing on the Accra Road, near the entrance to the University of Technology. Then after public preaching, Bible Correspondence Lessons and word of mouth, fifteen churches were started.

When Jerry Reynolds returned to the States in the summer of 1963, the Harold Derr family replaced the Reynolds. Later Dewayne and Jane Davenport returned to the States June 3, 1964. Since 1965 there have been six political coups in Ghana. In all of this, the church has grown steadily and in 2007, there are over 2,000 congregations, five preacher training schools and colleges as well as other great works. Ghanaian brethren are evangelizing and have started churches in 27 other countries. When they move about, they take the gospel and church with them.

At seventy-five years old, Jerry Reynolds returned to Ghana, December 2007 completing his sixty-fifth trip to Ghana. He plans to keep up his schedule of three trips a year to Ghana because he believes that God has given him his good physical health for that purpose. He is currently on the board of Ghana Bible College Foundation, Inc. a fundraising effort to provide funds for long-term needs.

On Jerry's sixty-fourth trip November 2006, he reported some exciting new developments. He visited a deaf school in Tongo. Stephen Owusu had taught the 210 deaf students Bible classes as well as cared for some of their health care needs. Stephen has had great success using the World Bible School lessons. Jerry visited the Academy for Christian Training project in Sumbrungu. This is about seven miles north of Bolgatanga. They have about 150 students studying the Bible and are in a construction project to build a church building as well as a school. In Yendi, which is 150 miles south of Bolgatanga, Jerry met with John Kanbonja. John is training about 60 preachers and leaders. John wants to be known as John the Idol burner. As he teaches people about the One Living God, John helps people burn their wooden idols.

Jerry O. Reynolds, 151 Shadow Pointe Circle,
Huntsville, AL 35806
Email: reynolds477@bellsouth.net (256) 726-8766

UPDATE ON THE GHANA BIBLE COLLEGE
The Gospel for Ghana Report September 2006

The Ghana Bible College was established in 1962 under the sponsorship of the Cedars Church of Christ in Wilmington, Delaware. The College will be celebrating its 45th anniversary at the November 2007 graduation. Dr. Samuel Obeng retired as Principal of the College in 2001 and Augustine Tawiah, a former student, took over as Principal in 2002.

The number of students enrolled in the college continues to increase and has reached a record of 80 students for the 2006-2007 academic years. The College offers two and three year programs in Sacred Ministry and Primary Health Care to provide additional training for preachers who have minimal financial recourse when serving local villages. The College employs a workforce of 21 people made up of 12 faculty and 9 administrative/support staff.

The College faculty and the students are involved in numerous outreach activities in Ghana. The College Principal, some faculty members and administrative staff assist local congregations throughout Ghana. The students go back to work with their congregations on weekends before returning to the campus on Sunday evening or Monday morning to attend lectures and classes. There is an estimated 2000 congregations now in Ghana. Our programs are designed to equip each student to preach the gospel and to enable each person to find a means of living and support for his family. We are seeking to recruit additional faculty so that we can offer a wide range of programs that will be accredited by the National Accreditation Board. We are developing our students for ministry as bi-vocational servants who are equipped for service in the church and community with a critical orientation towards faithfulness in their calling.

Woman's Ministry

We are experiencing an increasing number of women converts in most of our churches in Ghana. As a result, many congregations are responding with various programs to help these women to persist in faith. We have an active program here in Kumasi. The women in the metro area use our facilities at the Bible College for women's retreats, seminars, and prayer meetings.

Hope Foundation

The Ghanaian Church of Christ in Harlem, NY has helped to initiate a foundation for poor preachers in Ghana. They sent $30,000 to start the fund. The elders of the Bomso Church of Christ that meets at the Ghana Bible College campus oversee this effort.

Christ and Culture
Report by Augustine Tawiah, Principal of Ghana Bible College

"Upon switching on my phone in Accra, I immediately received a call from one of the students at the Bible College. Alex told me that his father had died ten days before and that he was in Accra to make arrangements for the burial and for the final funeral rites. But there were complications. Fact is, when Alex came to the Bible College, his father was not open to the idea. I therefore traveled with Alex up north to seek his father's approval and to indicate to his father that I will pay Alex's way through school. Alex had worked hard in his studies and had endeared himself to his school peers and faculty. The Dean of Students, brother Albert Boateng referred to Alex as my "son".

Alex is the oldest of five children and he must exercise leadership in the funeral of his father. Upon notice of his father's death, his immediate responsibility therefore was to meet his father's brothers and sisters and plan with them for a decent burial to be followed by a final funeral rite. Upon his arrival from the Brong-Ahaho Region to Accra, he was given a cold reception by these relatives. They said Alex's father had embarrassed them for not paying his monthly dues into the clan and not participating in the funeral of other members. Therefore, Alex and his siblings will not receive any favorable hearing concerning the father's funeral. Alex's father had worked as a policeman for thirty years. It was expected that when he was first hired, he would bring his first paycheck to the family house and they would perform some Voodoo rites for him. This was supposed to be his key to professional success in terms of rapid promotions and for protecting his pocket into prosperity. Although not a Christian, he still did not believe in the Voodoo and therefore did not go back to obtain the so-called blessing. But until he submitted to the spirit of his ancestors and libations and ablutions were made at the family shrine in the compound, his safety and success was not assured. Since he turned against these things, he had denounced his family heritage. Therefore, if any of his siblings were going to participate in his burial and final funeral rites, then he and his children should be re-incorporated into the family. The family will calculate the ages of Alex and all his siblings to determine how much they are in arrears since they reached the age of majority.

The "kind" Uncles of Alex indicated that he and his siblings together with the father were in arrears of $600. This amount must be paid with a sheep and four bottles of gin. They will use the gin and the sheep as sacrifice and libation respectively to pacify the ancestors and link them to Alex and his siblings. Until these things were provided and the rites completed, the brothers and sisters of Alex's father and the entire extended family will not participate in the funeral and neither will they allow his body to be buried.

Alex is a Christian and preparing for the ministry. How does he leave his siblings to participate in providing these elements for the ancestors and his father's family deity? Besides Alex does not have $600 to provide these things and then turn around to provide a decent funeral rite for his father. The father's family will not back down on these demands while young Alex is confronted with these crises in his young life. School is starting in three weeks and Alex must finish his school with a final exam. His siblings are also going back to school. My gut-feeling was to get your father's body and bury him where he died. The police will not release the body only to the nuclear family and if this was done at all, it would bring a permanent hostility between Alex's fathers' people and this would create additional problems. After thirty years with the police, Alex siblings under eighteen years will receive his benefits but this will be paid only when letters of administration are signed by the widow and the siblings of the deceased gentleman. If the wife pursues it alone with her children, the siblings of the deceased could institute legal action and this case could be locked up in the law court for a very long time. Meanwhile, the children's education will suffer, as the widow cannot support the children and all the younger children alone.

I have narrated the major points of this case to serve as an illustrative example of the never-ending tension between the gospel and the culture in my work in Ghana. I ask for your prayers for Alex and his siblings that God will soften the hearts of the late father's children and they may lay his body to rest."

The Gospel for Ghana Report
September 2006
Augustine Tawiah, Principal
Ghana Bible College
P. O. Box 3247
Kumasi, Ghana, West Africa
Email: nsempa@yahoo.com

Ghana Bible College Foundation
%Dan Boyd
7401 Maple Drive
N. Richland Hills, TX 76180
www.ghanabible.org
info@ghanabible.org

Cedars Church of Christ
511 Greenbank Road
Wilmington, DE 19808
(302) 994-3800

BIBLE TRANSLATORS

There are about 60 different language groups in Ghana. So it is crucial for a Bible to be in the language of the people. Three different groups have devoted their lives to accomplish this gigantic task.

Wycliffe Bible Translators

The oldest group is called Wycliffe Bible Translators. Dr. John Theodore Bendor-Samuel, widely known as JBS, as a leading linguist and specialist in African languages, pioneered Bible translation and literacy work in Africa.

"In October 1962 John Bendor-Samuel and his family took up residence and lived, first at Achimita (University of Ghana) and then in Nigeria (Enugu and Zaria) for the next 14 years. He directed the Summer Institute of Linguistics' (SIL) work in West Africa which expanded to Toga (1967), Cameroon (1968) and Ivory Coast (1968). In the 1970's as the Africa Area Director of SIL, he visited many countries, discussing with church and mission leaders the needs for future Bible translation work. He was responsible for starting work in Ethiopia (1974), Sudan (1975), Kenya, Burkina Faso, Senegal, Mali, Niger, Chad, Zaire, Morocco, Congo Brazzaville, Central African Republic and Mozambique. He made the initial allocations of SIL teams to each language, guiding the teams in their linguistic research, setting up and supervising the development of SIL branches in each country."

www.wycliffe.org
www.dacb.org/stories/ghana/bender-samuel_john.html

LUTHERAN BIBLE TRANSLATORS

A second group is called Lutheran Bible Translators. "Since 1964, missionaries supported by Lutheran Bible Translators have translated the New Testament into 25 languages that previously had no written form of God's Word. As a result, Scriptures are now available to seven million people who otherwise would not have access to the Good News of Salvation in the language of their hearts. There are 6,900 languages in the world. The 400 billion people who speak more that 4,500 of those languages still do not have access to the New Testament in their heart language."

News from Lutheran Bible Translators
303 N. Lake Street; P.O. Box 2050
Aurora, IL 60507-2050
www.Lbtgospelcom.net

PIONEER BIBLE TRANSLATORS

A third group is called Pioneer Bible Translators. Greg Pruett, the President reports that, "For over 30 years, we in Pioneer Bible

Translators have dedicated our lives to serving the Bible-less peoples of the world. We have the honor of translating the Bible together with 200 teammates for about 9 million people in 35 languages. Right now we are recruiting 200 more teammates to serve an additional 26 million Bible-less people in 34 more languages and establish four new fields over the next six years. As God blesses our current vision, in 6 to 8 years we will be translating the Bible for 35 million people in 69 languages."

USA Pioneer Bible Translators
7500 W. Camp Wisdom Road
Dallas, TX 75236
1(800) 332-8667
1(972) 708-7460
FAX 1(972) 708-7463
www.pbtusa.org

CANADA Pioneer Bible Translators
5300 – 53rd Avenue
Calgary, AB T3A 2G8
Canada

GHANA WEST AFRICA MISSIONS

"Ghana West Africa Missions, a non-profit corporation was established in 1987 for the purpose of serving people through drilling of water wells, the operation of Village of Hope, which includes the children's home, the clinic and the schools and to help the rural residents of Ghana to have healthier lives by teaching them simple lessons on nutrition, general health care, sanitation and other health related issues. In addition, the purpose includes helping people know the one true God and His Son Jesus Christ, so several evangelists are supported to go from place to place preaching the good news and baptizing people into Christ. Josiah Tilton is the Executive Director and he has been working on this project since 1977 and spent five years living in Ghana with his wife Boni and two sons.

In Ghana, most of the villages do not have a clean water source. The villagers have to go to ponds or rivers to fetch their water. The ponds are always polluted with bacteria such as cholera or E-coli. Almost always they are filled with Guinea worms and Schistosomes, which are parasites that cripple and debilitate those infected. Mothers, having no choice, go to fetch the unclean water and give it to their children, even though they know it will make them ill, or give them parasites. Without education or marketable skills, the mothers cannot get a job, and because one tribe cannot move onto the property of another, there is no where to go to relieve their family of the water problems. With generous gifts from brethren in America, in 1989 they began drilling water wells in rural villages, especially in Northern Ghana. Now more than 1 million people are drinking from these new wells."

Ghana West African Missions
P. O. Box 40
Searcy, AR 72145
(501) 207-1852
Josiah Tilton, Executive Director
Email: jtilton@gwam.org
www.ghanamission.org

Health care is vitally important to the 22 million people of Ghana. The life expectancy at birth in 2007 for the total population is 59 years. There is a high degree of risk of major infectious diseases of bacterial and protozoal diarrhea, hepatitis A, typhoid fever, malaria, yellow fever and schistosomiasis.

INTERNATIONAL HEALTH CARE FOUNDATION IHCF AFRICAN CHRISTIAN HOSPITALS

IHFC/African Christian Hospitals exists to support our established medical mission points in Nigeria and Ghana and to begin new mission points when appropriate opportunities arise. Presently they are involved in five medical mission efforts in West Africa—a clinic and two hospitals in Nigeria and two clinics in Ghana, one in the northern part of the country and on in the south.

In addition to the direct medical care offered through supported facilities, IHFC/African Christian Hospitals also hosts a medical mission's seminar each year in Dallas, Texas. This is the largest and oldest medical mission's seminar in the Church of Christ fellowship. Many organizations, ministries and individuals working around the globe attend to share ideas, information and fellowship.

YENDI WOUNDED CARE CLINIC

One of the fastest growing areas of the health care profession in the USA and Europe is wound care. Diabetic ulcers are painful and disabling and can even become life threatening, but until recently there has been little research in this area of health care. New scientific understanding of wounds and increasingly sophisticated products are being used to meet the needs of this vast patient population.

IHCF sponsors a Church of Christ Mission Clinic at Yendi, Ghana. When the Benskins, a missionary family arrived in Ghana in 1999 to assist at the Yendi Clinic, Peter Bombande was slipping into the clinic before it opened to do dressing changes on his many indigent wound patients.

He had some modern supplies donated from the USA, but mostly he used persistence and bed sheet bandages, triple antibiotic ointment, gloves and gauze were helpful but not always available. After Linda Benskin, R.N. arrived, she and Peter both modified their techniques as they worked together and learned from one another. After several dramatic successes with wound patients who were near death prior to coming to the clinic, the number of wound patients increased so much that they equipped a room especially for wound care. Peter and Linda continued to research and try new treatments for the wound patients, always including teaching and prayer. The Yendi Clinic is very unique because it serves as a medical missions point in an overwhelmingly Muslim area.

CHURCH OF CHRIST MISSION CLINIC
KUMASI, GHANA

The Kumasi Clinic shares a large campus in the city with Ghana Bible College and Bomso Church of Christ. The clinic operations include: an outpatient clinic, a Canadian missionary nurse, Avril Keoughan who provides regular mobile clinics to many villages to help sick people who are unable to come to Kumasi. She also maintains a primary health care training program.

NIGERIAN CHRISTIAN HOSPITAL

Nigerian Christian Hospital was begun in 1965 by missionary doctor Henry Farrar and others. Doctor Farrar's M.D. degree was awarded by the School of Medicine, University of Tennessee, Memphis on March 1954. He received the Verstandig Award upon graduation. This is awarded to the graduate who had overcame the most obstacles and voted most deserving of the degree by fellow classmates and the faculty. Dr. Farrar's wife Grace is a registered nurse. The Farrar's took their five children to Nigeria in 1964 to establish the hospital. In July 2007, Dr. Farrar, and Grace, well into their eighties, went back to Nigeria and Henry performed 100 surgeries.

Nigerian Christian Hospital has grown in every way through the years. Serving the Ibo tribe and located in Abia state, near the large southern Nigerian City of Aba. NCH now includes: 110 in-patient beds, 150 Nigerian workers, over 30,000 patients treated annually, seven full-time physicians, Dr. Bob Whitaker, missionary doctor, 2 full-time chaplains serving the sick and a housing compound with visitor's house. From the beginning of the medical works in Nigeria and in Ghana, the spiritual health of the patient has been stressed as greatly important along with the physical health. For this reason, at least one designated evangelist has been placed in each of the hospitals and clinics.

IHCF
African Christian Hospitals
102 N. Locust
Searcy, Arkansas 72143
(501) 268-9511
www.ihcf.net

THE SHIP OF LIFE

"On May 2, 2006, the "Ship of Life" was plying the Mekong River North of Phnom Penh in Cambodia about 90 miles where they were seeing an average of 100 patients per day. Project Director, Dr. Rick Northen along with Dr. Wattnach Chea treat people that have never seen a dentist or doctor and many have grossly exaggerated problems that come from having no access to health care and little knowledge of common preventative measures. Most have not ever used a tooth brush. Many women with thyroid glands the size of a cantaloupe, huge cysts and tumors, and every other chronic ailment imaginable come for help. Some can be helped, and others are assisted in accessing free surgery and treatment that is available if they can get to the city. The Lord's influence has been felt and

soon, we pray there will be churches up and down the river where the ship is working to spread good will and His love.

Partners in Progress
William E. (Bill) McDonough, Director
P. O. Box 13989
Maumelle, AR 72113
Bill McDonough
Email: pipwem@aol.com
www.partnersinprogress.org

RESOURCES FOR TRAVELING TO GHANA

Embassy of Ghana
3512 International Drive N.W.
Washington, DC 20008
Telephone (202) 686-4520

Consular Services
Ghana Permanent Mission to the U.N.
19 East 47th Street
New York, N.Y. 10017
Telephone (212) 832-1300

Honorary Consulate of Ghana
3434 Locke Lane
Houston, TX
Telephone (713) 960-8806

Center for Disease Control (CDC)
www.cdc.gov

Ghana West Africa
www.gwam.org

BIBLIOGRAPHY

Adamafio, Tawia,
Ghana Republic Souvenir, Ghana Information Services, Newman Neame Limited, London, Printed in Great Britain by Jordan-Gaskell Limited, London, 1962.

Adams T.D
A Ghana Geography. University of London Press Ltd., Warwick Square London E.C. 4, 1960

Antubam, Kofi,
Ghana's Heritage of Culture, Senior Art Master, Adrimota School Member, Arts Council of Ghana Member, Ghana Museum and Monuments Board Member, Koehler and Amelang, Leipzig, 1963.

Apraku L.D.,
A Prince of the Akans, Oxford University Press, Amen House, London E.C. 4, 1964.

_____*Airplane Accidents* 1959-1969,
http://www.emergency-management, Net/avi_acc_1959_1969. htm 3/2/2006

Ball, Edward,
Slaves in the Family, a Ballantine Book, Published by Random House Publishing Group, 1999.

Batten, T.R.,
Tropical Africa in World History, Book 1, The Foundations of Modern History, Second Edition, 1961, Oxford University Press, Amen House, London, E.C. 4.

_____*Bloody Sunday in Selma,* March 7, 1965, http:// en.wikipedia.org/wiki/1965.

Boateng, J.,
Ghana History – Ghana Languages, http://www.library.yale. edu.

Boyd, Dan, Ghana Bible College Foundation,
7401 Maple Drive, N. Richland Hills, TX 76180, www. ghanabible.org info@ghanabible.org

_____*Buddhist Monk Sets Himself on Fire.* June 11, 1963,http://www.multied.com/Vietnam/monk.html. 6/22/2006.

Cedars Church of Christ,
511 Greenbank Road, Wilmington, DE 19818, (302) 994-3800.

Center for Disease Control
CDC, www.cdc.gov.

Christian Chronicle,
Economic Turmoil Hinders Ghana Work, September 8, 1964, www.christianchronicle.org.

Consular Service, Ghana Permanent Mission to the U.N.,
19 East 47th Street, New York, N.Y. 10017, (212) 832-1300.

Debrunner, Hans W., Dr. Theology,
Witchcraft in Ghana, A Study on the Belief in Destructive Witches and its Effect on the Akan Tribes, Brown, Knight and Truscott Limited, London and Tonbridge, June 1961.

Embassy of Ghana, Information Section,
3512 International Drive, N.W. Washington, D.C. 20008, 1974, (202) 686-4520

Farrar, Grace J.,
Stand By and See What the Lord Will Accomplish, Star Bible Publications, 2002, pg.ix-x.

Fleming, Edith, Raymond Foundation,
Africa and Its People, Museum Storybook, Chicago Natural History Museum, 1961.

_____, *Ghana Became a Member of the Communist Family of Nations,* January 30, 1964, *Ghana Government Controls Tightened and Economy Falters,* November, 1964 New York Times.

_____,Ghana History, http://www.ghanaweb.com/Ghana Home Page/history/Timeline.php 3/2/2006.

Ghana Medical and Education Departments,
Ghana Nutrition and Cookery, Thomas Nelson and Sons, LTD, Parkside Works, Edinburgh 9, 1961.

Ghana Information Services,
Ghana at a Glance, Accra, 1963.

_____,Ghana West Africa, www.gwam.org

_____,*Ghana Yearbook,* A Daily Graphic Publication, 1964.

Haitz, Linn,
Juju Gods of West Africa, Concordia Publishing House, St. Louis, Missouri, 1961.

Holman, Mary and Tom, Lutheran Bible Translators,
News from Lutheran Bible Translators, July 2007, www. Lbt. gospelcom.net.

Honorary Consulate of Ghana,
3434 Lock Lane, Houston, TX (713) 960-8806.

_____,IHCF African Christian Hospitals, Volume 27, Number, Summer 2007, 102 N. Locust Street, Searcy, AR 72143, www.ihcf.net (501) 268-9511.

Kay, Barrington, B.S.C. (Econ) Phd., Senior Lecturer in Education, University of Ghana, *Bringing Up Children In Ghana, An Impressionistic Survey,* George Allen Unvin, LTD, Barrington Kaye, 1962, C. Tinling and Co., LTD, Liverpool, London and Prescot.

King, Martin Luther, *I Have a Dream,* speech August 28, 1963. http:// www.infoplease.com/Spot/civilrightstimeline1.html 6/22/2006.

Kyerematen, A.A.Y.,Director of the Ghana National Cultural Center, Kumasi, Ghana, *Panoply of Ghana,* Longmans, Green and Co., Ltd. 48 Grosvenor Street, London, WI Ghana Information Services, 1964.

Kyeretwie, K. O. Bonsu, Formerly of the Ghana National Cultural Center, Kumasi, Ghana, *Ashanti Heros,* Waterville Publishing House, Oxford University Press, Amen House, London, E.C. 4, Accra, Ghana, 1964.

_____, *Lumumba, Prime Minister in Congo Assassinated, Country split into four Fragments.* http://caxton.stockton.edu/ hod/decries/msn Reader$11 6/22/2006.

McDonough, William E. (Bill), Director, Partners in Progress, Spring 2007, P. O. Box 13989 Maumelle, AR 72113. www.part-nersinprogress.org. pipwem@aol.com

Meyerowitz, Eva L. R., *The Akan of Ghana, Their Ancient Beliefs,* Faber and Faber Limited; 24 Russell Square, London, W.C.1 printed in Great Britain by R. MacLehose and Co., Ltd, The University Press Glasgow, 1958. *The Divine Kingship in Ghana and Ancient Egypt,* Faber and Faber Ltd., 24 Russell Square, London, W.C. 1 1960

Pruett, Greg, President, Pioneer Bible Translators, September 2007. www.pioneerbible.org. USA Pioneer Bible Translators, 7500 W. Camp Wisdom Road, Dallas, TX 75236 1(800) 332-8667 www.pbtusa.org.

Radcliffe, A.R. Brown/Daryl Ford, Editors, *African Systems of Kinship and Marriage,* Published for the International African Institute by Oxford University Press, Amen House, London, E.C.4., First published 1950, Third Impression 1956.

Rattray, R.S., B.Sc.(oxon.) *Religion and Art in Ashanti,* Oxford University Press, Amen House, London, E.C. 4, First edition 1927, Reprinted 1954 and 1959.

Reynolds, Jerry O. 151 Shadow Pointe Circle, Huntsville, AL 35806, (256) 726-8766. reynolds477@bellsouth.net

Samuel, Dr. John Theodore Bender, Wycliffe Bible Translators, www.wycliffe.org www.dacb.org.

Segal, Ronald, *African Profiles,* Penguin Books, LTD. Harmondsworth, Middlesex, Penguin African Library 1962.

Tawiah, Augustine, Principal Ghana Bible College, *Gospel for Ghana,* September 2006, www.ghanabible.org.

Tilton, Josiah, Director Ghana West Africa Missions, March 2007. www.gwam.org. www.ghanamission.org.

West, April, *Ashanti Culture,* www.mnsu.edu June 2007.

Wolfson, Freda, *Pageant of Ghana, West African History Series,* General Editor: Gerald S. Graham, Rhodes professor of Imperial History, University of London, Oxford University Press, Amen House, London, E.C.4, West African Newspapers Ltd., 1958.

Printed in the United States
202290BV00004B/1-129/P